Glacier Bay

Icy Wilderness

Volume 15, Number 1 / 1988
ALASKA GEOGRAPHIC®

The Alaska Geographic Society

To teach many more to better know and use our natural resources

Editor: Penny Rennick
Associate Editor: Kathy Doogan
Editorial Assistant: Laurie Thompson
Review Editor: Ethel Dassow
Designer: Sandra Harner
Cartographer: Jon.Hersh

ALASKA GEOGRAPHIC®, ISSN 0361-1353, is published quarterly by The Alaska Geographic Society, Anchorage, Alaska 99509-3370. Second-class postage paid in Edmonds, Washington 98020-3588. Printed in U.S.A. Copyright © 1988 by The Alaska Geographic Society. All rights reserved. Registered trademark; Alaska Geographic, ISSN 0361-1353; Key title Alaska Geographic.

THE ALASKA GEOGRAPHIC SOCIETY is a nonprofit organization exploring new frontiers of knowledge across the lands of the Polar Rim, learning how other men and other countries live in their Norths, putting the geography book back in the classroom, exploring new methods of teaching and learning — sharing in the excitement of discovery in man's wonderful new world north of 51°16′.

MEMBERS OF THE SOCIETY receive *ALASKA GEOGRAPHIC®*, a quality magazine which devotes each quarterly issue to monographic in-depth coverage of a northern geographic region or resource-oriented subject.

MEMBERSHIP DUES in The Alaska Geographic Society are $30 per year; $34 to non-U.S. addresses. (Eighty percent of each year's dues is for a one-year subscription to *ALASKA GEOGRAPHIC®*.) Order from The Alaska Geographic Society, Box 93370, Anchorage, AK 99509-3370; phone (907) 258-2515.

MATERIALS SOUGHT: The editors of *ALASKA GEOGRAPHIC®* seek a wide variety of informative material on the lands north of 51°16′ on geographic subjects — anything to do with resources and their uses (with heavy emphasis on quality color photography) — from all the lands of the Polar River and the economically related north Polar Rim. We cannot be responsible for submissions not accompanied by sufficient postage for return by certified mail. Payments are made for all material upon publication.

CHANGE OF ADDRESS: The post office does not automatically forward *ALASKA GEOGRAPHIC®* when you move. To ensure continuous service, notify us six weeks before moving. Send us your new address and zip code (and moving date), your old address and zip code, and if possible send a mailing label from a copy of *ALASKA GEOGRAPHIC®*. Send this information to *ALASKA GEOGRAPHIC®* Mailing Offices, 130 Second Avenue South, Edmonds, WA 98020-3588.

MAILING LISTS: We have begun making our members' names and addresses available to carefully screened publications and companies whose products and activities may be of interest to you. If you would prefer not to receive such mailings, please so advise us, and include your mailing label (or your name and address if label is not available).

ABOUT THIS ISSUE: The core text for this review of Glacier Bay's icy wilderness comes from Rollo Pool of Juneau, Southeast representative for Alaska Northwest Publishing Company, and from the staff of The Alaska Geographic Society. We are grateful for assistance and review from Mike Tollefson, former superintendent of Glacier Bay National Park and Preserve; Gary Vequist, Greg Streveler, Bruce Paige and Scott Baker of the National Park Service staff at Glacier Bay; Larry Mayo of the U.S. Geological Survey; and Terry Chapin of the Institute of Arctic Biology. We thank Dave and JoAnn Lesh for recalling for us details of the history of Gustavus, and we appreciate the contributions of the many fine photographers who shared their images of this icy wonderland.

The Library of Congress has cataloged this serial publication as follows:
Alaska Geographic. v.1-
[Anchorage, Alaska Geographic Society] 1972-
v. ill. (part col.). 23 x 31 cm.
Quarterly
Official publication of The Alaska Geographic Society.
Key title: Alaska geographic, ISSN 0361-1353.
1. Alaska — Description and travel — 1959-
—Periodicals.
I. Alaska Geographic Society.F901.A266
917.98′04′505
72-92087Library of Congress
75[7912]   MARC-S

COVER: *A cruise ship passes the face of Margerie Glacier. According to the National Park Service, 146,967 tourists visited Glacier Bay in 1986.* (Clarence Summers)

PREVIOUS PAGE: *In the waning daylight, three hikers make their way along the shoulder of Black Mountain, above Muir Inlet and between Riggs and McBride glaciers.* (Clarence Summers)

STATEMENT OF OWNERSHIP MANAGEMENT and CIRCULATION

ALASKA GEOGRAPHIC® is a quarterly publication, home office at P.O. Box 93370, Anchorage, AK 99509. Editor is Penny Rennick. Publisher is The Alaska Geographic Society, a non-profit Alaska organization, P.O. Box 93370, Anchorage, AK 99509. Owners are Robert A. Henning and Phyllis G. Henning, P.O. Box 93370, Anchorage, AK 99509. Robert A. Henning and Phyllis G. Henning, husband and wife, are owners of 100 percent of all common stock outstanding.

ALASKA GEOGRAPHIC® has a membership of 14,131.

I certify that the statement above is correct and complete.
ROBERT A. HENNING
Chief Editor

Why? You might ask, do we publish another Glacier Bay book. Well, it could be honestly said the bay keeps changing . . . that is one of the exciting things about the dynamics of Glacier Bay glaciers, some coming, some going, new plants and life coming into being, others being crushed again into oblivion . . . but that is not why we have published still another. The fact is, an earlier *ALASKA GEOGRAPHIC®* volume was produced when park managers actually had known little about the seacoast side of the park . . . the turbulent seas of the North Pacific that lash the rocky shores from Cape Spencer north and west under the towering Mount Fairweather . . . and of that bay of ancient legend and many terrors, Lituya, where some of the earliest explorers saw for the first time Tlingit warriors and their villages, and where, likewise, Indians saw

Frenchmen and their great bird ships of white sail for the first time . . . magic places, dark places and wildly beautiful primeval places. This new edition of the *ALASKA GEOGRAPHIC®* will help to give you a broader understanding of how the park has developed over the years.

Sincerely,

Robert A. Henning,
President

Introduction

Almost nowhere else in the temperate world is so much water locked in glacial ice as in the northern end of Southeast Alaska now known as Glacier Bay National Park and Preserve. To cruise the bay is to marvel at the number and magnitude of the individual glaciers. To fly over the park is to be stunned by its diversity, its magnificence and the extent of the ice fields.

Certainly nowhere else is ice so well protected from human alteration. But the movement of a glacier, like the flow from a volcano, is an elemental force over which man has no control. Changes may be rapid; they may be imperceptibly slow, but they are constant, inexorable. Man can only observe and measure, marvel and speculate.

Glacier Bay is still emerging from the last Ice Age. At the time of the American Revolution, those fingers of salt water that now reach in among the glaciers were themselves under ice. Recession, today, is comparatively rapid. A change of a mere two degrees in world temperatures would accelerate or reverse the current melting trend.

Certainly, Glacier Bay offers spectacular scenery. What intrigues the observer as much or more, however, is its display of natural processes at work, ecosystems in the making, the progression from raw, newly exposed sand and gravel through lichens and mosses to pioneer plant species and, eventually, to climax forest. To cruise from Bartlett Cove north and west into any of the several inlets is to see reclamation in reverse, as each fraction of a mile takes one farther back in evolution of land recovery.

Walk along the lateral moraine of a glacier, and see dwarf fireweed flowering only feet from ancient ice. Peer into one of

A hiker enjoys a misty morning above Lituya Bay. In the distance, Lituya Glacier calves ice into the bay. (Clarence Summers)

Rays of light catch a chunk of aquamarine ice floating in Glacier Bay. (Don Cornelius)

the mysterious crevasses on the glacier's surface, and see rivulets of meltwater trickling into the bowels of the glacier, where it lubricates the friction of ice against bedrock. Drift through the floating ice off the face of a glacier, watch huge chunks of the face slough off into the water, and feel the motion as the waves rock the boat.

What will be there next year? And the next? A glacier that today fronts on tidewater may continue to advance, or it may recede and expose a wide strip of terminal moraine.

Perhaps the unpredictable but inevitable change, as much as the exhilaration of the scenic grandeur, is the fascination that brings the visitor back again and again to Glacier Bay.

Bergs calved from Margerie Glacier fill Tarr Inlet near the glacier's face. (Kim Heacox)

A canoeist paddles the calm waters of Wood Lake, south of the head of Geikie Inlet. John Muir named the inlet in 1879 for British geologist James Geikie, author of a book on the Great Ice Age. (Don Cornelius)

Glacial ice dwarfs a hiker near the Alsek River, at the northern boundary of Glacier Bay National Park and Preserve. (Karen Jettmar)

Facing southwest from Tarr Inlet, this aerial view looks over the West Arm of Glacier Bay and takes in Reid Glacier (right) and Hugh Miller Inlet and Gilbert Island (upper left). (Kim Heacox)

A sailboat catches the wind on a rare, crystal-clear day in Glacier Bay. (Clarence Summers)

Sunset illuminates mountaintops of the
Fairweather Range, to the west of Glacier Bay.
(Jim Shives)

Betty Fallon poses with four halibut taken from Glacier Bay. (Don Cornelius)

Bill Schafer, John Loudmell and Frank Murkowski clean shrimp on the deck of the Alaska Adventurer in Lituya Bay.
(Penny Rennick, staff)

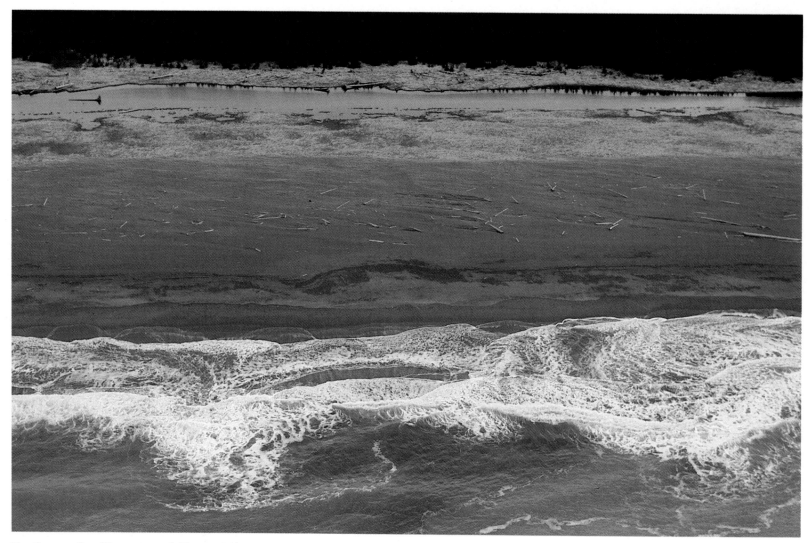

Frothy surf spills onto a driftwood-lined beach along the outer coast of Glacier Bay.
(Clarence Summers)

In Icebound Isolation

Glacier Bay National Park and Preserve consists of 5,100 square miles of snow and glacier ice, mountains and moraine, fresh water and sea. To put its size into perspective, it is slightly larger than our third-smallest state, Connecticut, yet slightly less than one percent of the total land in Alaska.

Although the area is attached to the North American mainland, it is in effect an island, accessible only by plane or boat. It is bounded on the south by Icy Strait and Cross Sound, on the west by the Gulf of Alaska, on the north by the Alsek River and a reach of British Columbia's massive ice field, and on the east by the near-impenetrable Chilkat Range and Takinsha Mountains. Traffic bound for Glacier Bay departs from Sitka, Hoonah or Juneau, Haines or Skagway on the north end of Lynn Canal, or Gustavus, on Icy Strait just outside the park boundary.

Of the 3.3-plus million acres now within Glacier Bay National Park and Preserve, 3,271,000 are park lands and 57,000 are preserve. Nearly 2.8 million acres of the total are designated as wilderness, the most restrictive classification of federal lands. The National Park Service, which has a year-round office on Bartlett Cove inside the park, manages all the park and preserve, but cooperates with the Alaska Department of Fish and Game, the National Marine Fisheries Service and the U.S. Forest Service on matters of mutual concern.

The mountain ranges of Glacier Bay inspire the loftiest of praise. French explorer Jean Francois de Galaup, Compte de La Perouse, who visited the area in 1786 recorded doubt that there could be a more

A group of kayakers moves through dense floating ice during an outing in Johns Hopkins Inlet, named for Johns Hopkins University in Baltimore.
(Hayden Kaden)

extraordinary place on earth. Scottish-American naturalist John Muir, who watched his first Glacier Bay sunset a century later, expressed the same sentiments.

Seasonal Calendar

Finding clear weather in Glacier Bay is possible but not expectable. It has a maritime climate, comparatively mild the year around, generally cloudy, with measurable precipitation on an average of two days out of three. This does not mean that the visitor who waits out two days of rain will be rewarded by a clear day. The third day may be dry but cloudy; it may keep on raining. Even in summer the really clear, sunny days come only three or four to the month, when the wind is from the north. The prevailing winds are from the south or southeast. They may blow for weeks without halt, bringing rain off the North Pacific and the Gulf of Alaska.

The average summer temperatures at Gustavus are from fifty to sixty degrees, rarely seventy or above. Winter temperatures there are twenty to thirty above, with a rare dip to minus ten.

Both temperatures and precipitation vary within the park. The outer coast, on the Gulf of Alaska, has milder temperatures, more clouds and fog, more rain but less snow than the southern and inland areas. Upper Glacier Bay gets the most snow, and temperatures there may be twenty degrees colder than those in Bartlett Cove and

A perch atop Black Mountain offers a commanding view of McBride Glacier (at left) and lower Muir Inlet (upper right).
(Clarence Summers)

The lush green rain forest along the outer coast of Glacier Bay provides a picturesque setting for a campsite. (Karen Jettmar)

Gustavus. At Park Headquarters in Bartlett Cove, an average of 75 inches of rain and 120 inches of snow fall each year. For comparison, Juneau, about 50 miles to the southeast, gets precipitation totaling 92 inches a year and Skagway, about 70 miles to the northeast, less than 30 inches.

Hours of darkness and daylight, on the other hand, are predictable. At the summer solstice, June 21 or 22, sunrise in Bartlett Cove is 3:51 a.m., and sunset, 10:09 p.m., which means 18 hours and 16.6 minutes of full daylight. From summer to winter solstice, daylight hours shorten so on December 21 or 22 the sun shines — if clouds don't hide it — for less than six hours.

During those long, dark winter months the land and its living things seem to sleep under new-fallen snow and the seals, gulls and eagles have the waters to themselves. Some of the small upper inlets almost always freeze over and pan ice may form in the upper reaches, but winds and tides keep the main bay open. Glacial melt slows or ceases, but the inexorable flow of the glaciers continues and the occasional calving of a tidewater glacier sends waves across the water and sound waves into the stillness. The throb of a fishing boat or the clang of a survey crew seems intrusive now.

Life quickens with the warming, lengthening days of spring. Bears, thin from their months of dormancy, some with the lately born cubs, leave their winter dens and start their constant search for food. Marmots and squirrels emerge. By mid-May the alders and cottonwoods are leafing out, and seals give birth to their pups on the ice floes. Resident birds are pairing and building nests. Flocks of migrant birds from wintering grounds perhaps thousands of miles to the south are competing for nesting space. Visitors start coming also. For those who wish to hike, spring is the best time, as water levels in the streams are still low and crossings are easier. In another month, melting snow will have swelled those streams and made them dangerous if not impossible to cross.

Flowers and shrubs begin to bloom. Birds fly back and forth, seeking food and carrying it to their nestlings. From mid-June the humpback whales come in to Glacier Bay to feed on shrimplike krill, and killer whales follow them to feed on anything they can find. Mosquitoes, too, appear in swarms, also feeding on whatever they can find, including human visitors, and in turn providing feed for the birds. July is the busiest month for both tourists and wildlife.

By mid-August summer activities are winding down. Grasses turn golden, flowers are going to seed, salmon return to spawn, and the bears leave the berry patches to feed and fatten on salmon. Lately hatched birds, now as big as their parents, are learning to fend for themselves. Soon the migratory species will leave the bay for the long flight to their traditional winter habitats. The southwest winds blow stronger, bringing cooler air and more rain. Darkness comes earlier each day, but there's compensation on the occasional clear evenings when the northern lights display their shimmering colors.

The autumnal equinox brings its characteristic storms and equalizes, briefly, the hours of daylight and darkness. Park facilities close soon afterward. Visitors, if any, must camp or stay at one of the inns in Gustavus. Once again the eagles, gulls and seals have the bay mostly to themselves.

Kayakers assemble their craft on the shore of Bartlett Cove. (Ernest Manewal)

Geographic Inventory

Although the trend of the terrain in Glacier Bay National Park and Preserve is definitely up and down, the peaks do not reach the heights of neighboring mountains in Alaska and Canada. Sixteen summits in the St. Elias and Wrangell mountains and the Alaska Range are higher than Mount Fairweather, 15,300 feet and highest in the park. Fairweather is, nonetheless, taller than any mountain in the other forty-nine states. In Europe, only Mount Blanc is taller and that by only 471 feet.

Highest of Mount Fairweather's neighbors are Mount Quincy Adams (13,650 feet), Crillon (12,728), Root (12,860), Salisbury (12,000), Lituya (11,924), La Perouse (10,728), Lodge (10,530) and Bertha (10,000), all in the Fairweather Range or the St. Elias Mountains, which parallel the Gulf of Alaska. They and the highest of the lesser peaks, some of them distinguished enough to have names of their own, wear perpetual mantles of ice and snow.

The Fairweathers front on the open sea and form the 125-mile west coast of the park. A forbidding coastline it is, with only one protected harbor on the hundred-mile stretch between Icy Point, to the south, and Dry Bay on the northwest park boundary. That harbor is Lituya Bay, which has its own peculiar hazards. It can be entered safely only at slack tide — about 15 to 30 minutes in every six hours. Count La Perouse, who surveyed Lituya Bay in 1786, narrowly escaped disaster at the entrance and did lose two longboats and twenty-one crewmen when they strayed too close to the entrance on an ebb tide. Lituya offers ample anchorage for a sizeable fleet, once it's inside, but even then it is not totally safe. The head of the T-shaped bay lies on a fault scarp, which slips at unpredictable intervals and produces major earthquakes. These in turn generate seismic waves of gigantic proportion, and any craft caught inside the bay has little chance of survival. (See page 34.)

La Perouse Glacier, about eight miles north of Icy Point, is the only one of the park's numerous glaciers to flow directly into the open sea. Its face, two to three hundred feet high and nearly vertical, serves mariners as a landmark on this stern coast where, more often than not, clouds hang low on the mountains.

Hikers take off across the flat shore along Glacier Bay's outer coast. (Karen Jettmar)

The Fairweathers form a barrier which forces the warm, moist air from the ocean to rise and drop its moisture as rain or snow, which in turn feeds the western glaciers within the park — Grand Plateau, Fairweather, Lituya, North and South Crillon, La Perouse, Finger, Brady and more.

From Icy Point south to Cape Spencer, southernmost point in the park, the coast is deeply indented. Boussole and Astrolobe bays, Dixon Harbor, Torch Bay and Graves Harbor afford safe anchorages in the lee of islands and headlands.

Around the broad hook of Cape Spencer,

Photographic opportunities abound in Glacier Bay, so visitors learn never to be caught without loaded cameras. Here, two kayakers on the Bartlett River commit a memorable scene to film. (Tim Steinberg)

on the north shore of Cross Sound, lies wide, blunt Taylor Bay, with the dirty face of Brady Glacier, about two miles wide, across its head. North Inian Pass leads from Cross Sound into Icy Strait, past Dundas Bay on the north or park side. Dundas is a two-armed bay, very deep in parts but very shallow in others, and the Dundas River,

A group of rafters enjoys a trip down the Alsek River, at the northern boundary of Glacier Bay National Preserve.
(Clarence Summers)

which flows into the northeast arm, carries so much silt that this bay may in time be filled.

Capt. George Vancouver, on his voyage in 1794, noted both Taylor and Dundas bays in his log and named Dundas Bay in honor of Henry Dundas, then treasurer of the Royal Navy. W.H. Dall of the U.S. Coast and Geodetic Survey named Taylor Bay nearly a century later, in honor of Mr. C.H. Taylor of Chicago.

On up into Icy Strait, a wide gap between Point Carolus and Strawberry Point, now better known as Point Gustavus, is the entrance to Glacier Bay itself. Beyond the entrance jogs the park boundary to exclude the settlement of Gustavus and its air strip. Around another long, broad point the park boundary turns northward up Excursion Inlet, a long, narrow, deep finger that pokes into the Chilkat Range. Midway along its east shore are the small settlement of Excursion Inlet, its salmon cannery and a seaplane wharf. There's scheduled floatplane service between Excursion Inlet and Juneau.

The eastern boundary of the park runs the length of the Chilkat Range, where the mountains rise to a mere five thousand feet but, even so, feed the eastern glaciers of the park — Casement, McBride, Riggs, Muir, Carroll. Between the park boundary and Lynn Canal, the corridor to Haines and Skagway, lies a sliver of Tongass National Forest and within it, the Endicott River Wilderness.

From the northern end of the Chilkat

The Beardslee Islands, dotting Glacier Bay near its southern end, are named for Navy Capt. Leslie Anthony Beardslee, who officially named the bay and was instrumental in producing the first map of it. (Rollo Pool, staff)

Range the park boundary curves northwestward along the crest of the Takhinsha Mountains, which face the Chilkat River valley. There it meets the International Boundary, follows it south and then west across the rugged British Columbia ice field, then north along the St. Elias Mountains to the lower Alsek River and downriver to Dry Bay.

The Alsek River and its major tributary, the Tatshenshini, make the only break in the coastal mountains between Cape Spencer and the Copper River. The Tatshenshini enters the Alsek some fifteen miles east of the international and park boundary. Together they offer a fine wild river experience.

Rivers within the park, all short by any standards, include the Excursion (24 miles long), Dundas (16 miles), Beartrack (15), Bartlett (14) and Salmon (13).

Glacier Bay itself, not only provides the name of the park and preserve; it literally cuts it in two. The head of Tarr Inlet, sixty-two miles from the mouth of the bay, meets the face of Grand Pacific Glacier near the Canadian border. For a time, about 1925 to 1948, Grand Pacific receded and exposed a strip of Canadian earth. Some Canadians believed they saw the exciting possibility of a new Canadian seaport hundreds of miles farther north than the ports of Prince Rupert and Stewart, at present the farthest-north West Coast Canadian ports. A party of Canadians, in fact, mounted an expedition in 1974 and planted the Maple Leaf at the head of Tarr Inlet, only to learn to their chagrin that Grand Pacific Glacier was again advancing and had already poked its snout nearly a mile into the United States.

Glacier Bay, a scant six miles wide at its entrance, broadens to ten miles in the next twenty-five or so, then forks. The east arm, Muir Inlet, with Adams Inlet branching off to the east and Wachusett Inlet to the west about midway, heads fifty-five miles from the bay's entrance. Riggs and Muir glaciers face each other across the head; McBride enters the inlet southeast of Riggs.

West Arm, longer of the two, has Tidal Inlet extending from its east shore, larger Queen Inlet farther on with the face of Carroll Glacier at its head, then narrower Rendu Inlet which meets the face of Rendu Glacier. Tarr and Johns Hopkins inlets fork northwest of Russell Island. Margerie Glacier enters Tarr Inlet from the west, only a mile or so from its head and the face of Grand Pacific Glacier. On a clear day, Margerie Glacier seems to be a gigantic stairway leading to the upper reaches of Mount Fairweather. Lamplugh Glacier enters Johns Hopkins Inlet from the south, near its entrance, several smaller glaciers meet its south shore, and the several branches of Johns Hopkins Glacier converge at the head of the inlet. Major inlets on the southwest side of West Arm are Reid, Hugh Miller and Geikie.

Land Types and Uses

From its saltwater shores to its ice-crusted summits, Glacier Bay presents a diversity of habitats and ecosystems. Mature forests interspersed with occasional marshes and bogs dominate the southern and western areas, from the rocky outside shores to timberline. Younger successional plant

A sign on the dock marks the headquarters for 5,100-square-mile Glacier Bay National Park and Preserve at Bartlett Cove, just inside the entrance to the bay. (Rollo Pool, staff)

Photographer George Wuerthner admires the breathtaking view from a vantage point above Hugh Miller Inlet. (Courtesy of George Wuerthner)

Hiker Aimee Youmans finds a cold but convenient resting spot among some of the area's icebergs. (Clarence Summers)

Various species of animals and upland birds find habitats to their liking.

Decades ago, before any of Glacier Bay was accorded national monument status, several entrepreneurs tried fox-farming on some of the islands. They were doomed to failure because, during the Great Depression, the market for furs almost ceased to exist. Prospectors did not overlook the bay in their quest for mineral wealth. None struck it rich, but there are still several valid mineral holdings within park boundaries, subject to strict access and development regulations. Park lands are off limits to current and future claim-staking.

Although land use restrictions differ within the park and the preserve, the aim of the Park Service is to keep the land in both categories as little developed as possible. Local residents are permitted to hunt and fish in the 57,000-acre preserve, which contains an air strip and a few private cabins. To protect nesting bird populations, access to some of the islands is restricted. Regulations also limit the number of commercial vessels allowed to enter the bay while whales are feeding there.

No change of status of either park or preserve lands seems likely in the foreseeable future.

A National Treasure

Fortunately, the unique values of Glacier Bay were recognized early on a national level, thanks largely to the popular writings of such men as John Muir, John Burroughs, W.H. Dall, and the report of the Harriman Expedition of 1899. President Calvin Coolidge, in 1925, signed into law a bill setting aside 2.5 million acres of land as Glacier Bay National Monument. The

communities are reclaiming patches of recently exposed earth among the glaciers within the bay. Upland shrubs, tundra and alpine meadows cover the slopes to the areas of perpetual snow and ice. Small lakes, fed by rains and meltwater, reflect the slopes and the clouds. Streams from rivulets to rivers come trickling or tumbling from higher ground and from under the glaciers.

presidential proclamation justified establishing the monument because the land offers:

A number of tidewater glaciers of the first rank in a magnificent setting of lofty peaks, . . . more accessible to ordinary travel than other similar regions of Alaska;

A great variety of forest covering consisting of mature areas, bodies of youthful trees which have become established since the retreat of the ice which should be preserved in absolutely natural conditions, and great stretches now bare that will become forested in the course of the next century;

A unique opportunity for the scientific study of glacial behavior and resulting movements and developments of flora and fauna and of certain valuable relics of interglacial forests;

Historic interest, having been visited by explorers and scientists since the early voyages of Vancouver in 1794 who left valuable records of such visits and explorations.

Acreage of the monument was increased in 1939 and again in 1978. Due in part to the efforts of homesteader Charles Parker, certain parts of Gustavus and Excursion Inlet were withdrawn from the monument in 1955. In 1980, with passage of the Alaska National Interest Lands Conservation Act, 585,000 acres were added, some of them designated as preserve, and the status of the unit was changed from national monument to national park.

A waterfall tumbles to an ice-blue pond in the Dundas Bay area of Glacier Bay National Park. (Karen Jettmar)

The Earth Never Sleeps

At one time, all of what is now Southeast Alaska was an underwater plain. During millions of years the land rose above sea level, and the mountains grew. Heat and pressure metamorphosed some of the older rocks into slates and schists. These processes continue. While some forces are building, others — wind, water, ice — are breaking down the landscape. It is slow work. As the ice melts, the land, relieved of the great weight, rebounds. Near Bartlett Cove and Gustavus, the rate of uplift is more than an inch per year.

Some of Glacier Bay's outer coast bedrock is made up of slivers carried hundreds of miles northward along three major lateral faults: the Chatham Strait, Border Range, and Fairweather-Queen Charlotte faults. That bedrock ranges in age from at least early Paleozoic (575 to 245 million years ago) to middle or late Pleistocene (1 million to 15,000 years ago).

The Fairweather-Queen Charlotte Fault nearly parallels the coast northward from Icy Point, across the head of Lituya Bay and on to Russell Fiord northeast of Yakutat. Along this line, one of the tectonic plates of the Pacific floor meets the North American plate. The lines where these plates meet are continually shifting. Some plates slide along each other; some slip under neighboring plates, descend slowly into the earth's fiery core, and melt. Some travel great distances, laterally, vertically or both. Certain rocks found at sea level near Icy Point, for example, are also found elsewhere along the fault, ten thousand feet up a mountainside. The outer coast is moving northwestward, past the inland mass — very slowly. It is conceivable that in twenty million years Los Angeles and its environs west of the San

Climbers Richard Steele and Mike Wild pause to rest atop Grassy Ridge, known locally as Mount Blunt, near Lituya Bay.
(Clarence Summers)

32

Evidence of one-time glaciation, a rocky spit protrudes into Goose Bay on the east coast of Muir Inlet. (George Wuerthner)

and earthquakes. Earthquakes cause seismic waves, which in mere minutes can alter a shoreline beyond recognition.

Earthquakes and Seismic Waves

Five major earthquakes during historic times have rocked the outer coast of what is now Glacier Bay National Park and Preserve, and the resulting seismic waves have stripped the shoreline forests to heights of sixty-five to almost two thousand feet. These quakes occurred in 1853, 1874, 1899, 1936 and 1958. Approximate heights of the ensuing waves have been determined by studying tree growth.

Lituya Bay, midway between Icy Point and Cape Fairweather and the only sheltered harbor along a hundred miles of coastline, has sustained most of the damage. It is a T-shaped bay with the Fairweather-Queen Charlotte Fault running along the crossbar of the T. A large tidewater glacier flows into each end of the bar, and a smaller glacier enters about midway between them.

French explorer La Perouse, first white man to visit Lituya, found two Tlingit villages inside the bay, one on Anchorage Cove inside long, narrow La Chaussee Spit, and one inside blunt Harbor Point. In fact, he bought Cenotaph Island from one of the Tlingit chiefs, and left a record of his visit somewhere among the rocks. Those records disappeared and so did the villages, presumably swept away in a seismic wave after the quake of 1853, or possibly 1874. According to Tlingit legend, some men from the village were out hunting sea otters. When they returned, they found devastation where their villages had been, and only one

Andreas Fault may arrive at the outer boundary of Glacier Bay.

Geological forces can also work with devasting speed. When a weak spot in the earth's crust can no longer resist pressure from below, a volcanic eruption occurs. When pressure at a fault scarp forces readjustments, they are made as tremors

Campers pitch their tent within view of Mount Crillon (12,728 feet), third-tallest mountain in Glacier Bay National Park. Crillon was named by La Perouse in 1786 for French military hero Gen. Louis des Balbes de Berton, Duke of Crillon. (Clarence Summers)

survivor, a woman who had been picking berries on the mountainside.

Whether anyone was in Lituya when the 1899 quake hit, no one knows. The events of October 27, 1936, are known. Prospector and trapper Jim Huscroft had lived for almost two decades on Cenotaph Island. Bernard Allen was with him that October, and they had fifty barrels of salted salmon in Huscroft's shoreside warehouse, awaiting shipment. Nick and Fritz Larsen, from Sitka, were trapping in the bay and living aboard their trolling boat, the *Mine*, anchored off the island below Huscroft's house. Huscroft was cooking breakfast when the earthquake hit. He and Allen fled to higher ground — altitude of Cenotaph Island is 320 feet — and escaped the ensuing wave. The house stood, but the warehouse and the barrels of salted salmon were washed away.

The wave dropped the *Mine* onto the bottom, then lifted her high on the backlash, but she rode it out with the Larsens aboard. Captain Tom Smith of the *Jacobi* reported four days later that timber from the devastated shores had spread over fifty miles of the Gulf of Alaska.

Huscroft stayed on in his cabin until his death on board the *Cenotaph* en route from Lituya Bay to Juneau in 1939. When Lituya Bay became part of Glacier Bay National Monument, it was closed to hunters and trappers and eventually to prospectors, but fishing vessels continued to use it for overnight shelter.

Summer 1958 brought more than the usual traffic to Lituya. Eight Canadian mountaineers had made the second recorded ascent of Mount Fairweather, and on July 9 were camped on the beach waiting for a Royal Canadian Air Force amphibian to pick them up next day. The pilot, concerned about an approaching storm, arrived at 6 p.m. on the ninth. The climbers broke camp in a hurry, and the plane departed. Ten other climbers, some of their supplies already stored in the Huscroft house, were to have arrived that day by boat. Fate chose to delay them. The bay was deserted, but not for long. The troller *Edrie* out of Pelican, with Howard Ulrich and his seven-year-old son, Howard Junior, aboard, came in on the ebb tide and anchored behind Harbor Point. They had finished dinner and turned in when the *Badger*, with Bill and Vivian

Swanson aboard, ran into the bay, picked up some floating glacial ice, then ran back and dropped the hook in Anchorage Cove. Not long afterward, Orville and Mickey Wagner aboard the *Sunmore* anchored nearby.

The earthquake started at 10:17 p.m. Howard and Sonny Ulrich woke in time to watch, spellbound, as Mount Fairweather and its lesser neighbors twisted and heaved. "They seemed to be suffering unbearable internal tortures," Ulrich reported in the October 1958 issue of *The Alaska Sportsman*, "then they spewed heavy clouds of snow and rocks into the air and threw huge avalanches down their sides."

Geologists later estimated that forty million cubic yards of dislodged rock and earth — enough to make a cube one thousand feet square and one thousand feet high — plunged into the bay. Ulrich continued:

I was petrified, rooted to the deck, then I looked over the shoulder of Cenotaph Island . . . with a deafening roar . . . a wall of water eighteen hundred feet high erupted against the western mountain. I saw it lash against the island and cut a fifty-foot swath through the trees at its center. Then I saw it backlash against the eastern shore, sweeping away the timber to a height of five hundred feet. Finally I saw a fifty-foot wave come out of this

Highest point in Glacier Bay National Park is Mount Fairweather (15,300 feet), which straddles the Alaska-Canada border. Capt. James Cook named the mountain in 1778, presumably because he encountered clear skies during his visit. The peak was first climbed in 1931 by Terris Moore and Allen Carpe. (Clarence Summers)

Peaks of the Fairweather Range tower over Lituya Bay, on the outer coast of Glacier Bay National Park. The largest wave known to man occurred here on July 10, 1958, when an earthquake shook an estimated forty million cubic yards of earth and debris into the bay.
(Karen Jettmar)

turmoil and move along the eastern shore toward me!

I began to move then, and move fast. First I got a life jacket on Sonny. Then I started the engine and tried to pull the anchor . . . it wouldn't budge. . . . Either the earthquake had wrapped the chain around a boulder on the bottom, or a crevice had opened and swallowed the anchor. . . . I let the chain run out, all of it . . . headed the *Edrie* into the incoming mountain of water, and waited for the impact.

The *Edrie* rode up the face of the wave. The anchor chain snapped. The end whipped back and wrapped itself around the pilothouse. The wave carried the boat over what had been timber-covered shore. It looked like the end for Howard Ulrich and his son. Howard Senior wrote:

> I wanted my wife back in Pelican to know where and how her husband and firstborn had been lost, and I grabbed my radiophone and yelled into it: "Mayday! Mayday! This is the *Edrie* in Lituya Bay. All hell has broken loose here." I faltered a bit, then . . . added, "I think we've had it. Good-bye."

In seconds the wave bounced off the eastern shore and started westward, carrying the *Edrie* with it. The water was full of icebergs, tree trunks and other debris. It was getting dark. Ulrich, using all the power of the engine, managed to avoid the heaviest flotsam and pull the *Edrie* out of the wave before she struck the west shore. He picked up his radiophone again and said, "I think we've weathered the worst." He didn't know whether either transmission was picked up, until the airways came to life with frantic inquiries about other boats. "All I can see," he responded, "is trees piled four feet high . . . all stripped clean of limbs and bark. If there were any boats behind the island, they've had it!"

The wave spent itself but great icebergs were churning over and over, grinding against one another. Any one of them "could have made kindling of the *Edrie*." Peeled tree trunks were like an immense logjam, running with the current.

"I had to get out of Lituya, and at once," Ulrich wrote. "Going out on the ebb was dangerous, very dangerous, but remaining in the bay was an invitation to complete destruction."

As Ulrich worked the *Edrie* through the debris toward the entrance, he saw a mast light outside. He grabbed his microphone and shouted, "For God's sake don't come in here! All hell's broken loose." George Bockman aboard the *Theron* responded by asking what Ulrich intended to do, then stationed his boat so his mast light served as a guide. The little *Edrie* took three solid combers over her house, but her engine did not falter. She reached the safety of the open sea.

Orville and Mickey Wagner on the *Sunmore* tried to run out of the bay ahead of the wave. They didn't make it. The wave picked up their big troller, swept her southward, and tossed her over Harbor Point. Would-be rescuers found only an oil slick where she went down.

Bill and Vivian Swanson, awakened by the turmoil, stood on the deck of the *Badger* in their nightclothes, immobilized by the spectacle. Said Bill later:

> The mountains were shaking something awful, with slides of rock and snow, but what I noticed most was the glacier, the one on the north, Lituya Glacier. . . . You can't ordinarily see that glacier from where I was anchored . . . it must have risen several hundred feet . . . it was jumping and shaking like crazy. Big chunks of ice were falling off the face . . . like a big load of rocks spilling off a dump truck . . . then suddenly the glacier dropped out of sight and there was a big wall of water going over the point.

The wave picked up the *Badger* and tossed her "like a matchstick" over La Chaussee Spit. "We went up over the trees, and I looked down on rocks as big as a house. . . . It felt like we were in a tin can and somebody was shaking it."

The *Badger* dropped stern-down. Before

The seventy-foot steamer Seaolin *of Juneau, shown here in 1895, served the Glacier Bay area at various times as a ferry, towboat and mail carrier, and to transport miners to and from Lituya Bay. She was built in 1883, in San Francisco. Legend has it that she was to have been named* Sea Lion, *but the painter visited a couple of waterfront bars on his way to do the lettering.* (Courtesy of Francis Caldwell)

she sank the Swansons managed to launch their punt and get into it. The oars were swept away. Bill tore off a thwart and paddled clear of the suction. Julian Graham aboard the *Luman*, one of several fishing boats that had come to help if they could, picked up the Swansons an hour and a half later, still in their nightclothes — all they had left. The *Badger* was their home as well as their livelihood.

In Yakutat Bay, some eighty miles to the northwest and outside the park, five people were picking strawberries on Khantaak Island. John Williams, Yakutat postmaster, and his wife, Dora, had just left the island. Janice Walsh Walton, part-owner of the Yakutat salmon cannery, and Mr. and Mrs. Robert Tibbles, employed at the CAA station, were preparing to leave when the earthquake started. No trace of them was ever found, and the water is now two hundred feet deep at the spot where they were standing.

Part of the fishing fleet had anchored in Dixon Harbor, northwest of Cape Spencer and about thirty-five miles south of Lituya Bay. John and Lillian Turner were there aboard their *Cameo*.

"We saw the whole mountain come down at Astrolabe Point," Mrs. Turner reported. "The tremors continued all night. It felt like our boat jumped twelve feet out of the water at one time. The dust and smoke from the mountains lasted for hours. It looked and felt like the end of the world."

The 1958 earthquake measured 7.8 on the Richter Scale. Later photos show the shores of Lituya Bay stripped to bedrock. On the northwest shore of Gilbert Inlet, above the glacier that Bill Swanson saw rising and falling, one lone tree stood below 1,720 feet. How many board feet of timber washed out of Lituya and spread across the North Pacific, one can only guess.

Bill and Vivian Swanson got another boat and kept on fishing. New growth has greened the scars on Lituya's shores. Fishing vessels still run the hazardous entrance to overnight in the bay, trusting to luck that the next great earthquake will not catch them there.

The Search for Buried Wealth

In the late 1800s, the lure of gold enticed thousands to Alaska and the Yukon. Prospectors and miners, singly, in pairs, in small groups, came north ahead of the masses who would, in the late 1890s, trudge over Chilkoot and White passes on their way to Dawson and the Klondike. Dick Willoughby explored the mountains on the west shore of Lynn Canal as early as 1879. The following year he assisted Navy Capt. L.A. Beardslee (1836-1903) with the survey that produced the first map of Glacier Bay and gave it an official name.

What little mineral exploration there was in Glacier Bay ceased in 1899, when a violent earthquake shook enough ice down into the bay to effectively cut off access for the next few years.

One of the mining legends of the area began about 1924, when prospector Joe Ibach and his wife, Muz, started their search for gold on Reid Inlet, in the West Arm of Glacier Bay. The Ibachs discovered two veins along Ptarmigan Creek, just northwest of the inlet, and staked the Monarch and Inca claims. Only then did they find out that federal status, stemming from the declaration of Glacier Bay as a national monument in 1925, restricted land use in the area. Ibach maintained his claims were legal, contending that one government agency said he could not work them and another said he would lose rights to the claims if he did not work them. Novelist Rex

Prospectors Joe and Muz Ibach pose at the door of their home on Lemesurier Island in 1954. The couple came to Glacier Bay in 1924 and lived off the land for more than thirty years. They built a cabin overlooking Reid Inlet in 1940, and, although the Ibachs lived on Lemesurier Island, they returned to the cabin every summer until 1956.
(Bruce Black; courtesy of Dave Bohn)

41

Beach wrote of Ibach's predicament and quoted Joe, "Muz and I steal off up there when we can and bootleg the ore out, like a couple of burglars. Our own ore! Imagine it! We don't dare tell anybody what we're doing so I dig the stuff and sort it, and she drags it down to the boat, a sack at a time, on a barrel-stave go-devil. It's an outrage!"

Ibach persuaded Beach to plead his case in Washington, D.C., and the next year the monument was opened to mining again. He argued that new jobs created by mining would save thousands of unemployed workers across the nation, and that development would not harm the monument's scenic beauty. Even with Glacier Bay once again open to claim-staking, there was no rush to the area. The gold just was not there. The Ibachs and partner Tom Smith split a grand sum of $26 after expenses and two years of work.

A stubborn survivor of early-day mining in the Glacier Bay area is the cabin Joe and Muz Ibach built on Reid Inlet. The Ibachs lived and mined in the area for more than thirty years.
(George Matz)

The Ibachs remained a fixture at Glacier Bay, living for years on Lemesurier Island in Icy Strait and always continuing their search for gold. Muz died in a Juneau hospital in 1959; Joe died the following year.

In 1928 prospector William Horsman settled in Dundas Bay with his wife. They were joined a few years later by Buck Harbeson, who worked Horsman's claims and spent the rest of his life, until 1964, at the bay.

Another mining partnership, Abraham Lincoln Parker and his son, Leslie F. Parker, in 1938 staked the LeRoy mines along Ptarmigan Creek, near the Ibachs' claims. The elder Parker, one of the founders of Gustavus, wanted a gold mine. For several years he worked on building a small, two-stamp mill at his home. When he finished the mill, Parker dismantled it, and he and his son towed it on a raft to upper Glacier Bay. They put in at the shore across from Ptarmigan Creek and began prospecting. Shortly afterward they dug into the Leroy gold vein, and moved the mill up Ptarmigan Creek, nearer the vein. Then they built an aerial tram and began mining. When Abraham Parker died in 1941, the claim was leased to six men who operated under the name of the LeRoy Mining Company. The present owner still occasionally works the mine.

Glacier Bay's best known mineral prospect is the nickel-copper deposit in the southwest corner of the park. A large mining company owns the rights to the deposit, called the Brady Glacier or Nunatak Lode, but has done no assay work for many years. Part of the claim lies under Brady Glacier, and access would require building a road from tidelands across park land.

In 1978 the U.S. Geological Survey

Three members of Arthur Mallory's party pose on the shore of Anchorage Cove, on Lituya Bay, on June 18, 1933. The men widened an old wagon road from the cove to Eagle River to accommodate this Model TT Ford pickup truck, which they brought from California. Although the miners departed after just a few discouraging weeks, they left the truck behind to be used by anyone willing to dry out the battery and put gas into the tank.
(Courtesy of Francis Caldwell)

published a report on mineral potential within the former monument. The report, which focused on Glacier Bay's interior regions rather than the outer coast, forecast low mining potential: "Glacier Bay National Monument contains few mineral deposits that are likely to be minable in the near future . . . some that would be minable with technological changes and many that are insignificant. The economic potential for petroleum, coal and other nonmetallic commodities . . . is low." Ilmenite (source of titanium used in paint pigments), magnetite, gold and platinum deposits are known along beaches of the outer coast where, as in Lituya Bay, some placer mining occurred between 1894 and 1917.

The 1976 Mining in the Parks Act repealed former mineral entry provisions within Glacier Bay. Park Service staff found 212 recorded claims but declared only two claim groups valid, the Brady Glacier deposit and the small gold claim on Ptarmigan Creek. Ruled invalid were, among others, 134 placer locations near Lituya Bay.

Ice Ages, Glaciers and Succession

Ice covers nearly ten percent of the earth's surface today. Only about three percent of Alaska is under ice, but that three percent totals almost thirty thousand square miles — enough to cover Rhode Island, Delaware, Connecticut, New Jersey, most of Massachusetts and all of Hawaii. Individual glaciers in Alaska number about a hundred thousand, from tiny cirques to massive Malaspina, the 850-square-mile piedmont glacier west of Yakutat.

For its part, Glacier Bay offers an impressive inventory of ice and snow: 16 tidewater glaciers, 30 or so valley or alpine glaciers, and about a dozen smaller, unnamed ones. Brady Icefield, the park's largest ice mass, covers 180 square miles and branches into nearly a dozen glaciers.

During the Pleistocene, or Great Ice Age, an ice sheet from 100 to 4,000 or 5,000 feet thick covered most of southcentral and southeastern Alaska. Most of Southeast Alaska may have slept through the Pleistocene under a blanket of ice a mile thick in places. This ice advanced and receded at least four times from about 1 million to about 15,000 years ago. The most recent advance, known as the Little Ice Age, occurred from about 1500 to 1920 AD.

Although some of Glacier Bay's glaciers are advancing, the trend today is toward rapid melting. When British explorer Capt. James Cook passed what is now Glacier Bay, in 1778, the ice extended beyond Bartlett Cove and almost into Icy Strait. A hundred years later, John Muir found the bay open thirty miles farther inland. Today boats cruise about fifty-five miles into the East Arm, Muir Inlet, and about sixty-two miles through West Arm to the head of either Tarr or Johns Hopkins Inlet.

Crevices in glacial ice show off its blue color, the result of all colors being absorbed except blue, which is transmitted. (David Koschmann)

44

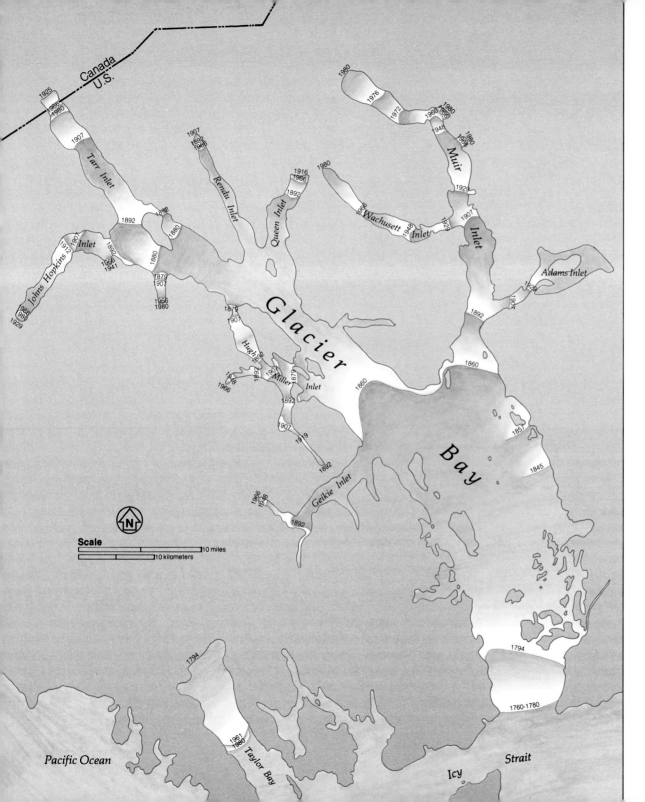

Ice-sheet advances and recessions have caused substantial fluctuations in sea level. During the Great Ice Age, when much of the world's water was stored as ice, sea level may have been three hundred feet lower than it is today. About seventy-five percent of all Alaska's fresh water is stored today as ice. If all of it were to melt, the world's current coastline would be inundated.

Atmospheric temperatures worldwide naturally influence the advance and retreat of ice fields. Since the 1940s the earth's air temperatures have fallen by about one degree Fahrenheit. Some people think this cooling trend will continue. Others predict that the greenhouse effect resulting from automobile and industrial emissions will produce a warming trend.

Glaciers form and grow when snow accumulates faster than it melts. Snowfall is heavy in Glacier Bay, as the prevailing southwest winds gather moisture in their sweep across the Gulf of Alaska, rise when they meet the high mountains along the coast, and drop their moisture as rain or, in the higher altitudes, snow — fifty feet of snow in some areas. At the latitude of Glacier Bay, 58° North, snow doesn't melt that fast. The weight of the fresh snow forces the air out of the residual snow, the individual flakes merge into dense ice crystals, and so glaciers are born. Accumulation continues, and gravity moves it downhill — a river of ice in slow motion. The weight and the friction scour the rock and sculpt the land, and in its flow the ice cracks and breaks, forming crevasses.

Glacier ice may look blue because it absorbs all other colors but transmits blue.

Ice positions in Glacier Bay from 1760 to 1980.

A pair of hikers looks at the terminus of Hugh Miller Glacier, named by John Muir for a Scottish geologist. The glacier, which once reached tidewater, has been steadily retreating. (Ernest Manewal)

Stumps are all that remain of an interstadial forest which occupied the area in the time between glacial advances. (Don Cornelius)

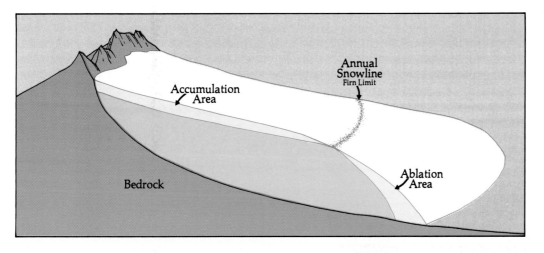

Annual Snowline
Firn Limit

Accumulation Area

Ablation Area

Bedrock

This theoretical cross section of a glacier shows the relationship of accumulation and ablation areas and the annual snow line (firn limit). Also shown is a plan view of a glacier with the ablation and accumulation areas outlined.

One method of determining the health of a glacier is by calculating the Accumulation Area Ratio or AAR. The AAR is defined as the ratio of the accumulation area to the total area of the glacier. The closer the AAR number is to one, the healthier the glacier.

Some does not look blue for the same reason snow does not; its surfaces are so rough that light does not penetrate; all light that strikes those surfaces is reflected. Much of the older ice is streaked with brown or gray by the dust blown onto its surface and the earth and rock picked up in its flow.

The eye does not detect the movement of a glacier, but move it does. A "galloping" glacier may surge forward as much as one to two hundred feet in a single day. A glacier that advances a hundred feet in a day can cover seven miles in a year! Gravity forces the ice to move, but the friction against the underlying bedrock slows the movement. Like a river of water, a river of ice flows unevenly, the main or central current flowing faster than the lateral ice, which is slowed by the added friction at the edges. The differences in the rates of flow cause more cracking and breaking. Crevasses may be a few feet deep, or as deep as the ice itself.

A skier looks into an ice cave on Geikie Glacier. Such caves, common along the edges of glaciers, are dangerous to explore.
(Clarence Summers)

Water trickling into the crevasses and seeping in from the lateral moraines tends to lubricate the bottom surface of the ice and speed its flow.

At the downhill end of a glacier is its zone of ablation, where melting and calving occur. Ice calved, or sloughed off, into Glacier Bay is an average of at least two hundred years old.

The ice rivers in Glacier Bay National Park and Preserve move independently. Of the sixteen tidewater glaciers, eight — Lituya and North Crillon in Lituya Bay; Reid, Lamplugh, Johns Hopkins, Margerie, Gilman and Grand Pacific in the West Arm of Glacier Bay — are advancing. La Perouse on the outer coast (the only glacier on the continent that calves directly into the open Pacific), Cascade in Lituya Bay, Hoonah, Toyatte and Kashoto in the West Arm and Riggs in the East Arm, are fairly stable. McBride and Muir, in the East Arm, Muir Inlet, are receding but at a much slower rate than formerly.

Tidewater glaciers begin to recede when they have pushed so far into deep water that the water undercuts the face. The snouts of advancing tidewater glaciers lie in shallow water, usually less than 250 feet deep, because they have built up platforms of moraine on which their snouts rest. If these glaciers begin to retreat, their fronts eventually back off the underwater moraines which support their weight, and their snouts fracture and crumble in deep water.

A glacier leaves unmistakable evidence on the landscape, from scars on scoured bedrock to outwash plain — the near-flat

Immense Brady Icefield, largest ice mass in Glacier Bay, covers 180 square miles and feeds nearly a dozen glaciers. (Rollo Pool, staff)

Turquoise water fills a kettle pond on the outwash plain of Geikie Glacier. Kettle ponds form when blocks of ice, buried in gravel and left behind after glaciers retreat, melt.
(Kim Heacox)

Multiple layers of compacted snow are easily seen in this iceberg in Johns Hopkins Inlet.
(Kenneth Parker)

expanse of terminal moraine composed of sediment carried along by the glacier. A kame is a short ridge of stratified glacial sediment. An esker is a long, narrow, usually sinuous ridge of stratified sediment left by a stream that flowed under, in or on a stagnant glacier. Drumlins are elongated hills of unstratified sediment, all tending in the same direction. Erratics are boulders, often huge, of almost angular shape, carried for perhaps great distances on or in glacial ice and usually identifiable because they are unrelated to the native rock. When blocks of ice buried in sediment later melt, they leave kettles, or potholes. Glacial dust, or flour, is bedrock pulverized by the movement of glacial ice.

Other natural phenomena accompany or result from glaciation. A nunatak, the name borrowed from Eskimo, is a peak surrounded by glacial ice. A sharp-crested nunatak may be called an arete or a horn. The slopes of a nunatak will show the scars of the ice long after the ice has melted. A cirque is a steep-walled bowl that holds, or once held, a hanging glacier.

By recognizing these phenomena, even a casual observer can determine whether one of the several ice advances reached a particular area — and if a change of climate were to cause all the ice in Glacier Bay to melt, it would leave ample evidence of what was once there to justify the name of the bay.

Chronicling the Changes

Henry Fielding Reid (1859-1944) rowed and backpacked his instruments throughout Glacier Bay in 1890 and 1892. A geologist and a professor at the Case School of Applied Sciences in Cleveland, Reid pieced together the jigsaw puzzle of Glacier Bay. [**Editor's note:** In some references, Reid's first name is Henry; in others, Harry.] He mapped the glaciers and found, among other things, that Muir Glacier at one time moved nearly ten feet per day at its center and about six feet at its margins.

William Skinner Cooper of the University of Minnesota first came to Glacier Bay in 1916. He saw the values in preserving the bay, and in 1923 recommended that the area be set aside as a national monument.

William O. Field, a geographer with the American Geographical Society, became spellbound by the bay in 1926. He believed that without consistent and accurate documentation, scientists could not see what was happening in the bay. He found that obtaining systematic documentation through the years was difficult, if not impossible, as advancing ice overtook his recording stations at several locations and at others, retreating ice rendered his observation points useless, or vegetation grew so fast as to obscure the view. Access, weather and the short field season required constant adjustment and innovation. Thanks to Field's groundwork, however, later field workers have been documenting the behavior of many of the glaciers. They have found that some, including Johns Hopkins and Grand Pacific, have both retreated and advanced during the last six decades.

Scientific investigations continue in Glacier Bay, where shifting ice creates a constantly changing laboratory.

A hiker stands high above surrounding Brady Glacier. The 175-square-mile glacier, which was calving into Taylor Bay at the time of Capt. George Vancouver's exploration, has now developed a large outwash plain in front of its terminus. (Clarence Summers)

FAR LEFT: *Riggs Glacier flows downslope to its terminus on Muir Inlet, off the east side of Glacier Bay. Riggs was examined in 1980 and found to be retreating.* (Tim Steinberg)

LEFT: *With a gigantic splash, ice calves from the face of Riggs Glacier. Falling ice and the resulting waves create hazards for boaters in Glacier Bay.* (Jim Shives)

Succession

Glacier Bay, where deglaciation began a mere two hundred years ago, provides a living laboratory for the study of plant succession. In Bartlett Cove, where earlier explorers would have seen raw earth, now stand mature Sitka spruce and western hemlock, and the forest floor is densely covered with the mosses, ferns and shrubs, including devil's club, characteristic of Southeast Alaska.

At the present head of Muir Inlet, there is nothing but newly exposed sand and rock. Between these two points, plant succession can be followed through all its stages. A

Wildflowers of every color and description push their way up through rocks and silt left when glaciers retreat. Flowers found in Glacier Bay National Park include (left to right) Siberian asters, Nootka lupine and paintbrush. (Left, Ernest Manewal; center, David Wm. Miller; right, Karen Jettmar)

56

feltlike black crust composed mostly of algae develops first. Mosses grow and help to stabilize the soil and hold moisture. Seeds and spores — windblown, carried in with the tide or on the furs of wandering animals, in bird droppings, even on campers' clothing and bedding — arrive and take root. The earliest plants, including scouring rush, dwarf fireweed, dryas, Sitka alder, willow, perhaps ryegrass along the beaches, are yellowish and stunted because glacial sediments are nitrogen-deficient. Alders and dryas have their own ways of taking nitrogen from the air and storing it in the soil where it is available to other plants. In five years a single rosette of dryas can become a mat a full yard in diameter. Scattered mats meet and form a carpet of dryas.

The leaf fall from alder adds as much nitrogen to the soil as a crop of alfalfa. In twenty years the alder will dominate, and soon become a near-impenetrable tangle. Its success is its own undoing, however, as it shuts off the light its own seedlings need for growth. The alder, having stabilized and enriched the soil, dies out and other plants flourish. Sitka spruce will dominate until western hemlock gets its turn, a century or two later.

Near the face of Muir Glacier as it was in 1890, John Muir had a cabin on bare, recently exposed moraine, with a fine view of the glacier and down Muir Inlet. Now, the face of Muir Glacier is about twenty miles farther inland and alders and spruce obscure the view from the cabin site.

Upslope plant succession differs somewhat from shoreside succession, and varies from slope to slope. In general, willow, soapberry, crowberry, blueberry and Labrador tea will be present. For reasons not fully understood

One variety of berry that thrives in Glacier Bay's moist climate is the plump red salmonberry. A member of the rose family, the shrub's pink flowers are followed in late summer by the juicy berries, popular for use in jams and jellies. (Kim Heacox)

but probably involved with variables in weather, plant succession in Tarr Inlet is far behind that in Muir Inlet.

Remnants of interstadial forests in Muir Inlet prove that plants have recovered the land at least once in prehistory, and suggest that the process may have been repeated many times.

Earliest Inhabitants, First Explorers

Natives

Although archaeological evidence indicates that people inhabited Southeast thousands of years ago, no one knows much about them, nor why there are huge voids in the human chronology of the area. More is known about the Tlingit peoples who until recently controlled most of Alaska's panhandle, part of the Gulf of Alaska and the inland trade routes.

Tlingit history, as noted in legends, speaks of the Little Ice Age that drove the people eastward from *Tcukanedi* ("Valley of the River of Grass") and finally across Icy Strait to the present-day site of Hoonah. In the lore handed down, a young girl who was confined during puberty called out to the glaciers in her loneliness. They responded by moving down the slopes and filling the flats, salmon streams and coastline.

The region's first known human inhabitants lived there ten thousand years ago, perhaps from the time the land awakened from the Great Ice Age. Archaeologists working at a site south of Excursion Inlet have found chopping tools, scrapers, flake tools and spearlike projectiles from this early period. How long people remained at this site is unknown, for after this early period there is an eight-thousand-year gap in our knowledge. Later artifacts — a house and microlithic and woodworking tools — have been dated to about the time of the birth of Christ. Another gap occurs, from almost two thousand years ago until about two hundred years ago, when the latest ice mass began to recede and the first white explorers came.

Archaeology owes much to Robert E. Ackerman for piecing together the

Natives hoping to sell their wares gather alongside a tour boat in Glacier Bay in this early 1900s postcard photo.
(Courtesy of Nicki Nielsen)

Indian Canoes, Glazier Bay Alaska.-

prehistoric puzzle from his surveys from 1963 to 1965. He and others identified more than sixty distinct sites or complexes from the past. Archaeologists have located numerous sites, including winter villages where the winds are mild and the bays are protected. The village site of Listi, in the Dundas River valley, had a small, permanent population to perhaps as late as the 1800s. Scientists have found no prehistoric sites along the rugged outer coast where the surf pounds, the cliffs are steep and sheltered bays are far apart. But Lituya and Dry bays, with their protected waters, supported permanent villages.

Within known time, Natives used the land within the park seasonally. Their lifestyles in Southeast revolved around small winter villages, hubs from which residents began seasonal hunting, fishing and gathering forays. Scattered fishing streams and hunting domains were divided like franchises among families within the settlements.

Just outside park boundaries, along Excursion Inlet, are two early village sites, one Native and one European, and a split log burial house. Near Point Couverden at the junction of Lynn Canal and Icy Strait, the Tlingits established year-round settlements. Today these camps, villages and graveyards lie in ruin. Early Natives also inhabited Port Frederick, location of the present-day Tlingit village of Hoonah.

It is obvious from the variety and abundance of natural resources in their territory and their highly developed art forms, that the Tlingits were a rich people when the first western explorers arrived in the late 1700s.

The White Man Arrives

Russian explorer Alexei Chirikov, in charge of the second ship under Vitus Bering's command on his voyage of discovery in 1741, skirted the Glacier Bay area before striking land farther south on the Panhandle. This expedition is credited with the discovery of Alaska, although on his 1728 expedition Bering's crew sighted the mainland near Bering Strait, and Chirikov made a landfall only a day before Bering sighted Mount St. Elias in July 1741.

By the late 1700s, other explorers fanned out along the North Pacific coast searching for new trade lands and a Northwest Passage to shorten trade routes between East and West. Englishman James Cook (1728-1779) cruised along this shore in 1778, when the United States was a mere two years old and when Glacier Bay was filled with ice all the way to Icy Strait. To Cook, the dent made by Glacier Bay would not have been worth a footnote in his log. He did, however, name 15,300-foot Mount Fairweather.

Prompted by Cook's reports, Frenchman Jean Francois de Galaup, Compte de La Perouse (1741-1788), sailed up the North Pacific coast and became the first to survey an area that is now part of Glacier Bay National Park. He arrived in Lituya Bay in July 1786, with two vessels, the *Astrolabe* and *Boussole*. His harrowing first entrance of Lituya was to be an omen of later events. In his log he wrote that in his thirty years at sea, he had never seen two ships so close to destruction.

Three small survey boats set out to take depth soundings of the bay. Although warned not to navigate near the treacherous spit that marked the entrance, they strayed too close, and two of the boats were sucked into the current and crushed. All twenty- one men in those boats perished. La Perouse and his crew erected a monument to the lost sailors on an island within the bay and named it Cenotaph, meaning empty tomb. [**Editor's note:** This earlier monument was destroyed by the elements, and a more permanent bronze plaque was erected on Cenotaph Island in 1985 to commemorate the two hundredth anniversary of the La Perouse expedition.]

La Perouse spent twenty-eight days with Natives of Lituya, and vividly described them and the bay's geography in *A Voyage 'Round The World 1785-1788* (1799):

We had already visited the head of the bay, which is perhaps the most extraordinary place in the world. To form an idea of it, it is necessary to conceive a basin of water, unfathomable in the middle, bordered by peaked mountains, of great height, covered with snow, and without one blade of grass to decorate this vast heap of rocks, condemned by nature to eternal sterility. I never beheld the surface of the water ruffled by a single breath of wind. Nothing disturbs it but the fall of enormous masses of ice, which frequently separate from five different glaciers, while the sound is re-echoed in the distant mountains.

La Perouse described the Natives of Lituya Bay as easily agitated and prone to combat

French explorer Jean Francois Galaup de La Perouse, hoping to find a northwest passage and establish a valid claim in North America for his homeland, landed at Lituya Bay in 1786. The map he made accurately placed five named glaciers in the bay's upper ends. This map has made it possible for scientists to note the changes in the positions of these glaciers through the years. (Alaska Historical Library; reprinted from *ALASKA GEOGRAPHIC®*)

on the one hand, while advanced in the arts, driven by ceremony and great lovers of games on the other. La Perouse records the following:

The men of this country bore holes through the cartilages of the nose and the ears, and append to them different little ornaments. They make scars on their arms and breast with a very keen instrument, which they sharpen by rubbing it on their teeth as on a whetstone. On occasions of high ceremony, they wear their hair long, braided and powdered with the down of sea fowl. A simple skin is thrown over their shoulders, and the rest of the body is left naked, except the head, which they commonly cover with a little hat, curiously woven; though sometimes they wear on their heads caps with two horns, eagle's feathers, and entire heads of bears fitted on the skullcap of wood. These kinds of headdresses are greatly diversified, but their principal object, like those of most of their customs, is to render them frightful, perhaps to awe their enemies.

La Perouse believed that the French could make money in the fur-trading industry at Lituya because this stretch along the Gulf of Alaska seemed to be unclaimed by various competing fur-trade empires. According to Alaskan historian Hubert Bancroft, La Perouse collected several thousand furs and sold them in Canton for between $10,000 and $20,000. Although La Perouse's optimism for fur trade in the

Bob Horchover, one of the organizers of the Lituya Bay Historical Society, holds the bronze plaque which members of the society placed on Cenotaph Island in 1985. The plaque commemorates the death two hundred years earlier of French seamen with explorer La Perouse, who were caught in the treacherous currents swirling around the bar at the entrance to the bay and drowned.
(Penny Rennick, staff)

region went unheeded by his countrymen, the Russians hunted sea otters there from 1796 to 1799.

In 1794 English explorer George Vancouver (1757-1798) and his crew charted

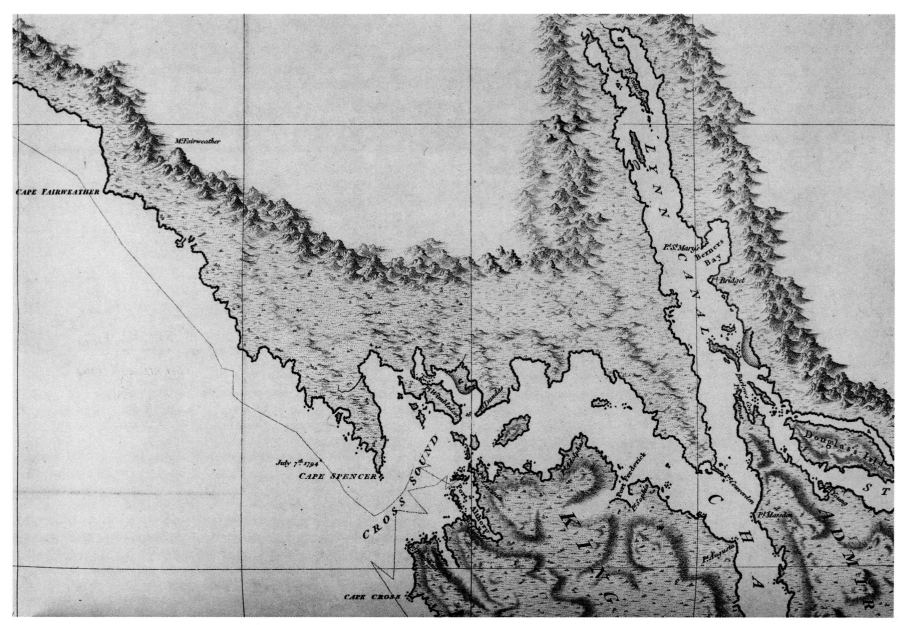

On this section of a map from Vancouver's voyage of 1794, Glacier Bay is a mere indentation in the coastline east of Point Dundas. (Courtesy of The Anchorage Museum)

Posing at John Muir's cabin on Muir Inlet in 1890 are (left to right) Muir, H.P. Cushing, C.A. Adams, H. McBride, Harry F. Reid, and (atop house) R.L. Casement. One of the bay's glaciers was named for each of these men.
(J.F. Morse photo; courtesy of Dave Bohn)

the coast south from Prince William Sound to Cross Sound and eastward toward Lynn Canal. They mapped in detail what later would be named Taylor and Dundas bays and Brady Glacier. Vancouver's map from that voyage shows no Glacier Bay, except for a small indentation in the coast between Point Gustavus and Point Carolus. The wall of ice still completely filled the bay. When John Muir (1838-1914) arrived in 1879, the ice had retreated thirty miles inland.

Nearly eighty-five years passed between Vancouver's visit and naturalist-explorer John Muir's October 1879 trip, the first of four he made to the area. Although Muir is generally credited with discovering Glacier Bay, Lt. Charles E.S. Wood explored several miles of the bay in 1877, two years before Muir's first journey, and joined a band of Natives on a mountain goat hunt.

Muir recorded most of his Glacier Bay experiences in *Travels in Alaska* (1915). On his first trip, Muir, his Indian guide Toyatte and missionary S. Hall Young persuaded a Hoonah Native by the name of Charley to lead their party deep into the bay.

Except for an exuberant Muir, the party traveled up the bay reluctantly. The others occasionally wanted to head back to safer territory, but not Muir. He had never seen such a strange and wonderful place, and each stroke of the paddle increased his desire to learn more about this icy world. On the second day of the trip, a Sunday, Muir wrote in his log:

The minister [S. Hall Young] wished to stay in camp; and so, on account of the weather, did the Indians. I therefore set out on an excursion, and spent the day alone on the mountain-slopes above the camp, and northward, to see what I might learn. Pushing on through rain and mud and sludgy snow, crossing many brown, boulder-choked torrents, wading, jumping and wallowing in snow up to my shoulders was mountaineering of the most trying kind. After crouching cramped and benumbed in the canoe, poulticed in wet or damp clothing night and day, my limbs had been asleep. This day they were awakened and in the hour of trial proved that they had not lost the cunning learned on many a mountain peak of the High Sierra. I reached a height of fifteen hundred feet, on the ridge that bounds the second of the great glaciers (Hugh Miller). All landscape was smothered in clouds and I began to fear that as far as wide views were concerned I had climbed in vain. But at length, the clouds lifted a little, and beneath their gray fringes I saw the berg-filled expanse of the bay, and the feet of the mountains that stand about it, and imposing fronts of five huge glaciers, the nearest being immediately beneath me. This was my first general view of Glacier Bay, a solitude of ice and snow and newborn rocks, dim, dreary, mysterious. I held the ground I had so dearly won for an hour or two, sheltering myself from the blast as best I could, while with benumbed fingers I sketched what I could see of the landscape, and wrote a few lines in my notebook. Then, breasting the snow again, crossing the shifting avalanche slopes and torrents, I reached camp about dark, wet and weary and glad.

. . . While I was getting coffee and hardtack, Mr. Young told me that the Indians were discouraged, and had been talking about turning back, fearing that

As word of the beauty of Glacier Bay circulated around 1880, tourists began flocking to the area. Here, in 1897, tourists use walking sticks to descend the moraine on Muir Glacier. (The Anchorage Museum)

I would be lost, the canoe broken, or in some other mysterious way the expedition would come to grief if I persisted in going further. They had been asking what possible motive I could have in climbing mountains when storms were blowing; and when he replied that I was only seeking knowledge, Toyatte said, ''Muir must be a witch to seek knowledge in such a place as this and in such miserable weather.''

Muir overcame their reluctance by telling them of his ten years' experience, wandering alone in the mountains in all sorts of

Photos of Glacier Bay's rivers of ice were popular with area visitors as well as armchair travelers throughout the world. Here, photographer Frank LaRoche's camera sits nearby as he peers into a large crevasse on Muir Glacier. (The Anchorage Museum)

and spire and dividing ridge of all the mighty host was spotless white, as if painted. It would seem that snow could never be made to lie on the steepest slopes and precipices unless plastered on when wet, and then frozen. . . . In the evening, after witnessing the unveiling of the majestic peaks and glaciers and their baptism in the down-pouring sunbeams, it seemed inconceivable that nature could have anything finer to show us.

The foursome toured Reid and Carroll glaciers and into the eastern arm, witnessing what later would be called Muir Glacier, while Muir himself made notes and sketches. The thickening ice in their path constantly reminded them that the safe canoeing season was past. Had they become locked in this wasteland, they would never have gotten out. Near the end of October they returned to the village at the mouth of Glacier Bay and rejoiced with the Natives, who heralded the return of Charley. They had reason to celebrate, since many Hoonah Natives had been lost in the icy bay during seal hunts.

Alaska's magnetism drew Muir north again the following year, 1880. This time, however, he traveled to Glacier Bay in the summer. He studied Muir Glacier and climbed into some of the alpine meadows of larkspur, columbine, gentian, fleabane, wintergreen, bluebells and anemone, compelling him to recount:

weather and always having had good fortune on his side. With their renewed confidence in him and his luck, they continued up West Arm, and again Muir climbed to get an overview:

The view to the westward is bounded and almost filled by the glorious Fairweather Mountains, the highest among them springing aloft in sublime beauty of nearly sixteen thousand feet, while from base to summit every peak

The first vessel to schedule tours into Glacier Bay was the sidewheeler Ancon, *shown here at Muir Glacier in 1887.* (The Anchorage Museum)

In this postcard scene created for the Alaska-Yukon-Pacific Exposition of 1909, an excursion steamer approaches for a close look at the ice in Glacier Bay. (Courtesy of Nicki Nielsen)

A violent earthquake in 1899 shook loose tons of ice in Glacier Bay, making many of the inlets impassable. The steamer Spokane *gained fame in 1907, when she was the first tour boat after the earthquake to approach within a mile of the face of Muir Glacier.* (Courtesy of Nicki Nielsen)

In June 1945, 700 German prisoners of war arrived at the Alaska Barge Terminal on the shore of Excursion Inlet, charged with the task of tearing down the $18 million military base constructed less than two years earlier. The prisoners lived in relative comfort during their four-month stay in Alaska. The photo below shows the POWs returning to their stockade for a lunch break; at right, prisoners patronize the camp's "Kantine." (Both photos, Alaska Historical Library; reprinted from *The ALASKA JOURNAL®*)

The very thought of the Alaska garden is a joyful exhilaration. Though the storm-beaten ground it is growing on is nearly half a mile high, the glacier centuries ago flowed over it as a river flows over a boulder; but out of all the cold darkness and glacial crushing and grinding comes this warm, abounding beauty and life to teach us that what we have in our faithless ignorance and fear called destruction is creation finer and finer.

By 1880, word of Glacier Bay had spread, attracting hundreds of tourists. In 1883 Capt. James Carroll and his pilot, Dick Willoughby, sailed the mail steamer *Idaho* north of Willoughby Island to become the first vessel to explore this far up the bay. Carroll named the largest glacier and east arm after John Muir. The following year, the captain cruised to Muir Glacier in the sidewheeler *Ancon*, initiating a fledgling tourist industry which grew with the spread of Muir's popular writings about this icy wonderland. Captain Carroll arranged for a small dock and a boardwalk to be built across the moraine of Muir Glacier so his passengers could get a closer look at the ice face.

Those who visited the area in 1890 could get their natural history straight from the old master himself for John Muir returned for his third trip that summer. He spent much of the season operating out of a cabin he built on the east side of Muir Inlet. On this trip Muir almost met his fate. Traveling solo and pulling a sled, he skirted Adams Inlet, hiked over Casement Glacier and climbed to the summits of several peaks. After days of bright sunshine, the glare from the ice blurred his vision. Temporarily blinded, he fell into a crevasse. But his good luck prevailed, and he made it back to safety.

The year 1883 also saw the opening of the first cannery on Bartlett Cove to exploit the sockeye run in the Bartlett River. The cannery joined with Dick Willoughby's trading post to mark the beginning of commercial enterprise in the bay. Pioneer Willoughby was certainly one of the first white men to live in Glacier Bay, where he piloted vessels heading up the bay in addition to operating the trading post.

Many of the glaciers that Harry Fielding Reid, George Wright and Muir studied are gone today or greatly reduced in size. But all who made their mark in Glacier Bay during this period — Capt. James Carroll, skipper of several passenger boats; Dick Willoughby; L.A. Beardslee; scientist G.W. Lamplugh and others — are remembered. Glaciers, islands and mountains of the bay carry their names.

Muir returned for his last visit to Glacier Bay in 1899. By then in his sixties, Muir traveled with Edward H. Harriman's scientific expedition. Some of the nation's top researchers joined the expedition, which made fifty scientific stops from Seattle to the Bering Sea.

One of the earliest residents of the Glacier Bay area was Jim Huscroft, who made his home in Lituya Bay from around 1917 until his death in 1939. Although he came looking for gold, Huscroft soon gave up on mining and built a permanent home on Cenotaph Island, where he maintained a large vegetable garden and ran a fox farm with Ernie Rognan. The foxes were allowed to run free on the island, but most died from disease in the early 1930s and the venture was discontinued by 1935. Huscroft, remembered as a kind and generous man who loved visitors and always welcomed them with food and a place to stay, is shown here in 1930 with his pet fox Tuffy. (Bradford Washburn, Boston Museum of Science; courtesy of Francis Caldwell, reprinted from *Land of the Ocean Mists* [1986])

The Marine Environment

No trip to Glacier Bay is complete without the sight of a whale spouting or a seal with its pup or a salmon jumping. A stroll along the tidelands of Bartlett Cove can also give visitors a sense of the area's rich marine environment.

For the most part, the visitor will find nothing there that cannot be found elsewhere in Southeast Alaska. In fact, many of the intertidal creatures inhabit several areas of the North Pacific coast. Mussels, cockles, scallops, clams and many other marine species that live in Glacier Bay also can be found as far south as California, as far west as the Aleutian Islands, and as far north as the Arctic Ocean.

Five species of Pacific salmon come in to spawn in the rivers and lakes. King, tanner and Dungeness crab inhabit waters within the park. Commercial fishermen harvest salmon, halibut and crab, and Glacier Bay is becoming increasingly popular for charter sportfishing.

Residents of the fishing communities of Hoonah, Gustavus, Elfin Cove and Pelican take their catches from waters in and adjacent to the park. In the Icy Strait and Glacier Bay areas, commercial fishermen land about one million to two million pounds of salmon each year. Inside park boundaries, fishermen take about 500,000 pounds of halibut and more than 400,000 pounds of crab each year. Pink, spot and coonstripe shrimp are found in abundance in park waters, but because they are food for endangered humpback whales, the Park Service prohibits their harvest within Glacier Bay itself.

Commercial trollers also fish along the outer coast of Glacier Bay, and at times pot

Harbor seals bask in the sun on Sealers Island, in Muir Inlet. These seals, the most common marine mammals in Glacier Bay, feed on a wide variety of fish and shellfish.
(Kim Heacox)

A commercial set-net fisherman weighs a load of salmon taken from the Alsek River-Dry Bay area. (Clarence Summers)

A Glacier Bay halibut fisherman seems happy with his catch. About one-half million pounds of halibut are taken within the park each year. (Clarence Summers)

Bill Bushey and John Loudmell sort clams, one of several seafoods available in Lituya Bay. (Penny Rennick, staff)

Pink, coonstripe and spot shrimp are found within Glacier Bay National Park waters, but because they are food for the endangered humpback whale, the Park Service prohibits harvest of shrimp inside Glacier Bay itself. Shrimping is allowed in outer coast bays such as Lituya. (Karen Jettmar)

Dungeness crabs, one of Glacier Bay's shellfish inhabitants, are found in shallow water from the Aleutians to Baja California, and are the basis for an important commercial fishery. (Jim Shives)

Once hunted to near extinction, sea otters are making a comeback in the Glacier Bay area. These members of the weasel family feed primarily on shellfish, each consuming twenty to twenty-five pounds of food a day.
(Howard Robinson)

A blood star clings to the rocks in a Bartlett Cove tide pool. More than fifty species of sea stars occur in Alaskan waters; most stars have between five and twenty-four arms, or rays, depending upon species. Sea stars can regenerate rays lost to injury or accident.
(Kim Heacox)

and trawl shrimpers have fished Lituya Bay. The shrimpers are not there every year, however. Set gillnet fishermen catch salmon in Dry Bay at the northern edge of Glacier Bay National Preserve. Coves along the outer coast shelter fishing boats during stormy weather and offer calm anchorage for fish-buying vessels during the fishing season.

Visitors traveling up the bay to the head of Johns Hopkins or Muir inlets often see harbor seals with pups from May to August. Steller sea lions have at least two haul-out areas on the outer coast. They also gather near Point Adolphus on Icy Strait in June and later in the fall, and in 1987 were noted in the strait all summer long. [**Editor's note:** While not technically within Glacier Bay National Park and Preserve, Point Adolphus is on the south shore of Icy Strait, opposite the entrance to Glacier Bay, and waters off the point are considered an integral part of Glacier Bay's marine environment.] Dall porpoises are uncommon in Glacier Bay; their more secretive cousins, harbor porpoises, are numerous. A few dozen sea otters, recently reintroduced to the area, have been recorded near the mouth of Glacier Bay, but this species has yet to make much progress in moving up the bay.

Minke and killer whales are common in Glacier Bay's inland waters in summer; giant blue, fin, gray and sperm whales swim along the outer coast. According to National Park Service biologists, killer whales have been

Steller sea lions cavort on the rocks along the outer coast of Glacier Bay National Park. These huge mammals have at least two haul-out areas on the outer coast, and they also gather near Point Adolphus on Icy Strait.
(Karen Jettmar)

Smallest of baleen whales in the northern hemisphere, minkes reach a maximum of 30 feet in length and weigh about 9 tons. They feed on krill and several kinds of fish. (Illustration by Donald Sineti)

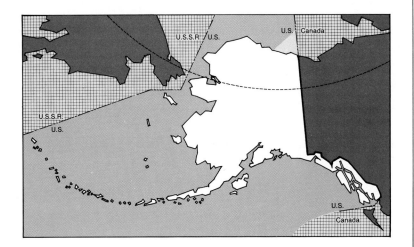

The initial caption for the photo at right referred to the humpback whale's great appetite and referred to "the bubble net theory" wherein whales were declared to circle a school of herring, surround them with a net of bubbles and properly balled in a small area, the herring were then proper mouthfuls for humpback whales rushing up through them from underneath.

We apologize for foisting this theory on the reading public in an early ALASKA GEOGRAPHIC®, Whales & Whaling. We had told an editor involved not to print it, but he did and we've been apologizing ever since, because in our considerable experience it just isn't likely. There are bubbles there, yes, and there are humpback whales circling the herring school, much like cowboys rounding up the steers. As many as five or six humpbacks will circle herring and close them into a tighter and tighter ball, swimming in tighter and tighter circles, creating a chartreuse sea of bubbles that might be fifty feet or so across and as deep, then suddenly from underneath, up come the three or four giants of the deep, mouths wide open, herring spilling out, crashing back down together, often lolling there, seeming to savor the last juicy morsel. Bubbles? No question about there being bubbles, but with monsters churning their flukes in high-speed turns under and around a zillion or so herring churning in flight, everybody's making bubbles. We've had the good fortune to see this happen many times and have been close enough above an impending burst of broaching whales through a school of herring to actually dimly see the thrust of those giant tails. As to their speed at this point, all I could say is they were really moving!

—Robert A. Henning
President
The Alaska Geographic Society

(Robert E. Johnson, reprinted from ALASKA GEOGRAPHIC®)

The efficient coordinated attacks on much larger prey have earned killer whales their nickname of wolves of the sea. Adult males may reach a length of 30 feet. (Illustration by Donald Sineti)

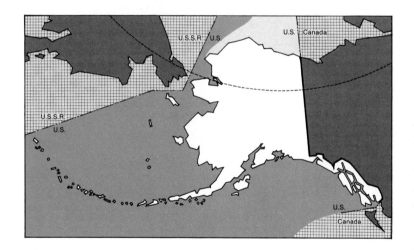

seen with increasing regularity in Glacier Bay, and the area has become one of the best places in Southeast to view this species.

The marine mammal now receiving the most official attention in Glacier Bay is the humpback whale, a forty- to fifty-foot baleen whale which migrates to Southeast each summer from wintering grounds off Hawaii or Baja California. The sudden departure of seventeen of the twenty humpbacks feeding in the park's inland waters in 1978 caught the attention of the public and marine mammal biologists throughout the country.

Humpback whales have been using Glacier Bay as a summer feeding ground for many years. They migrate north each summer after mating and giving birth to their calves in warmer waters. In Alaska, humpbacks feed primarily on krill (a shrimplike invertebrate), capelin, herring and sand lance, consuming enough in one season to sustain themselves through the remainder of the year.

The North Pacific population of humpbacks is about 1,200 to 2,000, 200 to 400 of which spend their summers in Southeast. Others head farther north into Prince William Sound, off the Aleutian Islands and into the Bering Sea. A few have been known to winter over in Southeast, but most head south. Many have become regulars at Glacier Bay; one whale, nicknamed Garfunkle by biologist Charles Jurasz, has made Glacier Bay his summer home since his birth in 1974.

When the humpbacks abruptly left the bay in 1978, officials became concerned. In that and previous years, cruise ship traffic to the area had increased dramatically, peaking in 1977 at 139 vessels.

The departure of the whales generated several questions and two hypotheses: either the whales left because of a decline in food, or because of the increase in the number of ships and boats visiting the bay.

In 1979, the National Marine Fisheries Service, charged with protecting marine mammals, issued a biological opinion stating that "if the amount of vessel traffic in Glacier Bay was allowed to increase without limit or if the existing restrictions on the operation of the vessels within the bay were removed, the associated disturbance would be likely to jeopardize the continued existence of the southeast Alaska humpback whale stock." The agency recommended that more research be done to better understand the complex variables affecting whales, that boat traffic be limited to the 1976 level and that boat navigation be restricted.

The National Park Service, which manages park lands and adjacent waters, subsequently adopted these recommendations and wrote regulations stipulating use limits for cruise ships and private boats. In addition, except for commercial fishing or charter boats actively fishing, no motorized vessel may intentionally position itself within one-half mile of a whale, and no vessel can pursue a whale. Within waters whales are known to use, all vessels larger than sixteen feet in length and not engaged in fishing must follow a mid-channel course at speeds of ten knots or less.

Cruise ship companies had been marketing Glacier Bay as one of their stops and thought the regulations would hurt sales. Instead, the demand for cruises, particularly to Southeast and Glacier Bay, continued to rise. To meet this demand, cruise lines began bringing in larger ships, vessels that could carry up to twelve hundred passengers.

In 1981, federal agencies launched systemic studies of the humpbacks of Glacier Bay. Acoustical researchers measured underwater sound levels of passing ships and ambient noise characteristics of the bay. Other researchers investigated whale prey, measuring zooplankton and the abundance of small fish at feeding sites. Others explored how whales respond to the presence of vessels.

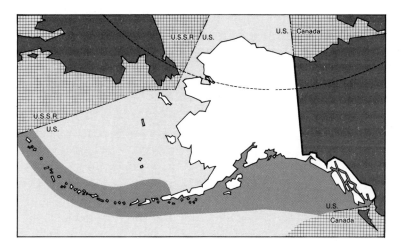

A much-desired attraction for boaters in southeastern Alaska and along the state's gulf coast, humpbacks are easily identified by their huge flippers and ventral grooves. They reach a length of 53 feet. (Illustration by Donald Sineti)

Through this research, scientists have learned that availability of food affects the distribution of whales present in the bay. Boat traffic can disturb the whales, but they are able to go to other areas of Southeast to feed. In other words, when given a choice, whales will go where there is more food and less noise and interruption.

Dr. Scott Baker, a National Park Service marine biologist, has studied the distribution and abundance of whales visiting Glacier Bay since 1981. He has found that the number of whales in the Icy Strait-Glacier Bay region has not varied significantly from year to year, although the number actually entering Glacier Bay's inland waters has fluctuated. Both areas have seen an increase since the early 1980s in the number of humpbacks feeding there. The overall local summer humpback population, including those animals that simply spend a day or two and move on, is between forty and fifty animals. Of this total, twenty-eight adults and four calves were counted in 1986 in Glacier Bay, twenty-nine adults and three calves in 1987. Many of these individuals remain to feed in the area all summer long.

In November 1987 the Park Service announced its decision to allow a seven percent increase in the number of vessels permitted to enter Glacier Bay in 1988. The decision was based on research which indicated that the increase would not pose any significant risks to the whales.

The Royal Princess carries tourists into Johns Hopkins Inlet. Concern about the effect of traffic on whales feeding in Glacier Bay has brought about restrictions on the number of cruise ships which can enter the bay.
(Rollo Pool, staff)

Wildlife

At least 220 species of birds and 24 of mammals share the icy realm of Glacier Bay. For the birdwatcher, the bay offers an abundance of forest, shore-space and seabirds.

Walkers exploring the trails through mature forest around Bartlett Cove and on the park's southern and western fringes may catch glimpses of blue grouse, three-toed woodpeckers, several thrushes including robins, varied and hermit thrushes, black-capped chickadees, fox sparrows and ruby-crowned kinglets. In forest openings they will hear the whir of a rufous hummingbird's wings.

Shorebirds take to the barren gravel plains and estuaries. Species residing in or migrating through Glacier Bay include lesser golden plovers, semipalmated plovers, oystercatchers, greater and lesser yellowlegs, dunlins and several other kinds of sandpipers. Northern phalaropes are one of the most numerous bird species in the park in late summer.

Abundant open water and coastline provide suitable habitat for seabirds. North and South Marble islands have the largest seabird colonies within Glacier Bay proper and are closed to foot traffic during the nesting season, as are other islands and islets with seabird colonies. But kayakers and tour boat passengers can get a good look from the water at tufted and horned puffins, pelagic cormorants, pigeon guillemots, oystercatchers and glaucous-winged and herring gulls. Rafts of marbled and Kittlitz's murrelets float in the bay. In winter at least 15,000 common murres can be counted there.

In midsummer, hidden bays shelter Vancouver Canada geese, while migrating

A white-tailed ptarmigan pauses on a rocky slope in Glacier Bay National Park. These birds, smallest of all ptarmigan, turn pure white in winter. (Don Cornelius)

Easily recognized because of its striking plumage and conspicuous crest, the Steller's jay inhabits coastal forests. (David Wm. Miller)

A colony of black-legged kittiwakes nests on a sheer rock wall in Glacier Bay. (Kim Heacox)

A flock of female harlequin ducks swims along a rocky shore in Glacier Bay. These ducks are common throughout Southeast Alaska. (Donald Cornelius)

An American black oystercatcher looks for food among the rocks of Goose Cove in Glacier Bay National Park. These birds live along rocky shores, on reefs or on islands, nesting in beach gravel. (Kim Heacox)

Clumsy and slow-moving, the porcupine's defense is its thick coat of barbed quills. The quills detach easily from the porcupine's skin, and the barbs work them into the flesh of the victim. (Karen Jettmar)

sandhill cranes stop to rest and feed on the open marshes near Gustavus.

Alpine areas of Glacier Bay are home to ptarmigan, snow buntings and redpolls. Farther downslope, in the alder-cottonwood thickets, flit Wilson's, orange-crowned and yellow warblers.

Bald eagles, ravens and crows are found throughout the park, wherever food and shelter are available.

Less is known about bird life on the rugged outer coast, but northern fulmars and species of shearwaters, petrels and gulls have been recorded there.

Brown and black bears and moose roam the park, mixing with such smaller mammals as wolverine, wolf, coyote and marmot. Steep slopes above the bays, such as the flanks of Mount Wright (5,139 feet), provide escape routes for mountain goats. In addition to an introduced population on Willoughby Island, Sitka black-tailed deer are found in forests on the park's southeast margin. Waterways and saltwater bays offer suitable habitat for river otters and mink.

As may be expected, areas of recent glacial retreat are the least likely to support plant and animal life. Surface materials at glacial fronts eventually make rootholds for lichens and mosses, horsetails and fireweed. In time, alders, willows and cottonwoods move in. Birds use these areas infrequently, but in summer months they provide refuge for some mammals.

And the ice itself is not devoid of life. Minuscule black worms, known as ice worms

A black bear stops for a snack on a grassy slope near the shore of Bartlett Cove. These bears, which usually weigh one to two hundred pounds, are found over about three-fourths of Alaska. (Karen Jettmar)

and the subject of many Alaskan myths, appear as tiny threads. These worms eat algae, bacteria and other organic matter, and in turn provide nourishment for passing snow buntings.

Moose have made a recent comeback in the park. Once rare, they now have established populations along Muir and Adams inlets. Although some moose were seen along coastal portions of the park in the 1930s, no evidence indicates their existence in inland reaches of Glacier Bay until two decades ago. Biologists speculate on the source of these moose; the most likely entry is from the Chilkat River drainage near Haines. The moose may have

A curious marten peers down from its treetop perch. These animals, members of the weasel family, can be found throughout most timbered areas in Alaska. (Shelley Schneider)

been drawn by an abundant supply of willow, their favorite food, which thrives in many areas after the retreat of the glaciers. As willow gives way to other plants during the process of succession, patches of the moose's main staple may diminish, and thus so will the moose population. In the meantime, the arrival of this largest member of North America's deer family has attracted wolves; several packs now claim hunting territories that include the moose range.

One of the smallest residents of Glacier Bay National Park is the ice worm. These worms eat algae, bacteria and other organic matter, and in turn provide nourishment for passing birds. (Kim Heacox)

In coastal areas, mountain goats such as this mother and kid are often seen at low elevations, particularly in winter and spring. Females usually give birth to a single kid in May or June; the kids can keep up with the parents when only hours old. (David Wm. Miller)

Gustavus

When the first settlers came to the flat plain along the north shore of Icy Strait, they named the area Strawberry Point because berries grew abundantly there. William H. Dall, an early Alaskan scientist, had already named one of the area's prominent land features seven miles down the coast Point Gustavus in honor of the King of Sweden. About 1940, residents of the area decided to adopt the name of the point, and the fledgling community became Gustavus.

The first residents to stake their claim along this stretch of Icy Strait, including Ernie Swanson, Vern Henry, Orville Rude and Jack Davis, were fishermen who decided in 1914 to turn their longlines into plowshares. As one of them said, "All seafaring men seem to get that notion sooner or later." The land surrounding Point Gustavus was an obvious choice . . . it is flat.

The early arrivals rolled up their sleeves and got down to the business of farming. By 1917, Swanson said it looked as if they might make some money from their crops:

Everything grew well that year. In addition, the war had started, prices were going up and there was a big demand for vegetables in Seattle. There was no dock at Strawberry Point and we had to carry the produce out to a skiff, put it aboard the *Mildred*, then haul it to Hoonah. Our first shipment consisted of 150 sacks of rutabagas . . . loaded aboard the steamer *Alki*. The next day, which was November 1, she struck a reef at Point Augusta [on the northeast coast of Chichagof Island] and stayed there.

The cargo was salvaged, however, so

Gustavus residents enjoy alternative modes of transportation for getting around their community. (Tim Steinberg)

our shipment was not lost but merely delayed. It finally was transferred to the *Mariposa*. A couple of days later, on November 18, the *Mariposa* hit Strait Island Reef in Sumner Strait. She became a total loss, as did our rutabagas.

We got ready another shipment, laboriously hauled it to Hoonah, and hoisted it up onto the dock to wait for another steamer. The weather turned cold, there was no warm storage on the dock, and the whole lot froze. It was discouraging but we figured we could still make wages for our labor with the produce we had left. We got it sacked and ready to go, stacked above the high tide line at Strawberry Point and ready to load the next morning. Something happened to the tide that night. It came up much higher than it was supposed to and by morning our shipment was watersoaked and worthless. I lost interest in farming right then and have never regained it. —Ernie Swanson, *The ALASKA SPORTSMAN*, October 1964

There were others, however, who had better luck, and did not have to go through the distribution tangles of getting produce from Alaska to the Lower 48. From the initial efforts of a few hardy pioneers, a tiny farming community emerged at Strawberry Point, and its farmers were able to raise some cattle, berries and produce for sale to nearby canneries.

Many of these early settlers stayed for a year or two, then left. One family who remained operated a sawmill. Abraham Lincoln Parker and his wife and sons operated the mill, cutting rough lumber for the canneries. The Parkers, who later staked the LeRoy Mine, came to Strawberry Point in 1917 from Shotter's Mill on Excursion Inlet.

As visitors look on, charter fishing guide Jim Mackovjak of Gustavus fillets a halibut. (Rollo Pool, staff)

When Glacier Bay National Monument was established in 1925, and later during the military buildup of World War II, Gustavus residents worked for the National Park Service and the Civil Aeronautics Authority (CAA). The Army Air Force built an emergency field at Gustavus during the war. Afterward residents worked for the CAA maintaining the airstrip, and helped with construction of the ten-mile road which in 1955 linked Gustavus with Bartlett Cove.

Excursion Inlet was the site of a major military camp completed in November 1943. The military command planned to barge supplies up the Inside Passage and transfer them to ocean-going convoys at the inlet for the run across the Gulf of Alaska to the

In 1985, Gustavus residents Al and Annie Unrein converted their home, located on their working farm, into the Glacier Bay Country Inn. On the farm they grow hay, vegetables and herbs for the inn and for commercial sale. (Both photos by Rollo Pool, staff)

Fishing boats, part of the community's small commercial fleet, line up along the Salmon River at Gustavus. (Rollo Pool, staff)

Aleutians Islands. By the time the camp was completed, however, the Japanese had been driven from the Aleutians, and German prisoners of war were brought in to dismantle the camp.

Several years ago Al and Annie Unrein won the right to purchase a 160-acre agricultural parcel near Gustavus. They built roads and a bridge, cleared a large tract of land and dug ditches so the lowlands could drain. They planted crops but, after harvesting, found they were able to sell the fruits of their labor only to Gustavus residents, local restaurants and a couple of businessmen in Juneau. Because of the cost of getting their crops to paying markets, they discovered, as had the early Strawberry Point farmers, that distribution was difficult without a developed transportation network. The cost of air freight alone was more than what some of the Unreins' produce sold for in Juneau stores. In 1985, the Unreins decided to convert their home to the Glacier Bay Country Inn, a part of their working farm, one of only a few in Southeast. They still grow hay, vegetables and herbs for their own use and for commercial sale.

Commercial growth for the area today centers around tourism. Many Glacier Bay-bound visitors overlook Gustavus, thus missing an opportunity for a close look at a growing rural community and a chance to stay at one of the inns for which the area is becoming widely known.

Gustavus, population 218, is off the beaten path for Southeast tourists, who cannot drive there nor arrive by ferry. But the town has an airport terminal and paved runway, with daily jet service to Juneau, Anchorage and Seattle during the summer. Commuter and charter planes carry passengers and freight all year long. In summer, fast catamarans link Gustavus with Juneau, forty-eight miles away.

From the air, one sees that Gustavus is laid out like farm country. Some of the original 160-acre homesteads now are being broken into smaller parcels as demand for land there increases. The town has no centralized business district; at the airport there are a couple of businesses, and a little way down the main road, a post office and school. Farther along there are a lumber store and a cafe, then a lodge and an inn. Another half mile farther are a general store and another cafe. Residents in 1986 established a library.

For a city dweller, distances between stores may seem a hassle, but in Gustavus clocks do not seem so important. The pace is refreshingly slow, one reason visitors repeat Gustavus on their Alaskan itineraries, time after time. Most of the inns lend bicycles to their patrons, and many locals have horses. Three-wheelers, pickup trucks and bicycles dominate the gravel roads, yet the traffic can hardly be considered heavy.

Some of the finest Alaskan cooking can be found in the area. The Gustavus Inn, one of the original homesteads and an inn since 1965, offers cooking classes in the spring. By early summer, most of the food that owners Dave and JoAnn Lesh serve their guests comes directly from nearby gardens and seas — from the lettuce, radishes and kelp pickles to crab, salmon and halibut.

Visitors and residents gather their fishing equipment and head for the dock at Icy Passage or walk down the road to the Salmon River to throw in their lines. Some commercial fishermen operate out of Gustavus, although the tiny fleet does not have the catch of larger Southeast ports.

Residents of Gustavus appreciate their mountain-fringed plain, the bountiful sea at their doorstep and the icy wonderland that is their neighbor to the north and west.

Dave Lesh is right at home in the kitchen of Gustavus Inn, where he helps prepare meals from locally caught seafood and the homegrown vegetables for which the area is well known. (Penny Rennick, staff)

Warm weather means time to bring out the water slide at the home of Dave and JoAnn Lesh at Gustavus. Enjoying the fun (front to back) are Jonathan Tanner, Sean Hall, Anna Lesh (in red), and (in back, left to right) Ben Lesh, Casey Hall and Joe, Jeff and Dan Lesh.
(Penny Rennick, staff)

Transportation, Accommodations, Services, Cautions

How to Get to Glacier Bay

You can get to Glacier Bay National Park and Preserve only by boat or plane. The one road into the park is from Gustavus, itself accessible only by boat or plane. Alaska Airlines has daily jet flights from Juneau to Gustavus from mid-May to mid-September. A bus meets the flight to transport passengers to Park Headquarters at Bartlett Cove. (There is no landing field in the park, though of course floatplanes land on the bay.)

Gustavus has floatplane service the year-round, but no scheduled ground transport to the park in the off-season. Hoonah, across Icy Strait on Chichagof Island, has thrice-weekly ferry service, and floatplane charter service to Bartlett Cove and Gustavus.

For information about tour-boat service from Juneau, write the Juneau Chamber of Commerce (address below). For information about Alaska cruises that include a day in Glacier Bay, and about scheduled or charter flightseeing, write the Park Superintendent (address below).

Private boats may enter the bay, but by permit only between June 1 and August 31 (apply to the Park Superintendent, by mail, not more than two months in advance). Diesel fuel and gas are available in Bartlett Cove. There's tie-up space for refueling only, but safe and unrestricted anchorage nearby. Skippers should inquire at Park Headquarters about off-limit areas, and should not attempt to navigate the bay without charts (available at Park Headquarters).

There is no scheduled service to other points in the park, and air drops of people and freight are not permitted. Floatplane charters can be arranged from Sitka,

Two visitors to Glacier Bay National Park load their folding kayaks onto a floatplane at the end of a wilderness trip. (Ernest Manewal)

Hoonah, Juneau, Haines, Skagway and Yakutat. One attractive though costly possibility is to charter a flight to Lituya Bay, hike to Dry Bay, and be met there by prearrangement.

Where to Stay

Glacier Bay Lodge in Bartlett Cove, a concession open from mid-May to mid-September, has motel-style rooms, dining room, bar, snack-type groceries, showers, laundromat and telephones available to nonguests.

Accommodations in Gustavus include two inns, a lodge and rental cabins.

Accommodations in Gustavus include David and JoAnn Lesh's Gustavus Inn, one of the original homesteads and an inn since 1965. (Rollo Pool, staff)

The Park Service maintains a 35-unit no-fee campground in Bartlett Cove. Facilities include a bear-proof food cache, fire pits and firewood but no place to store gear while you're absent. Reservations are not required; stay is limited to 14 days.

Camping is permitted in the back country, but carry out your refuse and bury human waste. Select a camp spot well above tideline — the tidal range is 25 feet — and away from game trails. Don't expect to find firewood. Bring a camp stove and white-gas container to be filled at the Bartlett Cove wharf (it's illegal to carry gas aboard a plane). Bring plenty of insect repellent and fine-mesh mosquito netting.

How to Get Around in Glacier Bay

A concessionaire-operated tour boat leaves Bartlett Cove daily and explores the West Arm. Another boat departs three times weekly on an overnight cruise in the West Arm. The overnight cruises should be booked well in advance. Arrangements can be made for drop-offs and pickups for an added fee. Larger cruise ships from Seattle or Vancouver, British Columbia, visit both arms, but these are prearranged, package cruises, not the tours that originate at Bartlett Cove.

Excursion-boat or plane trips, or a combination of boat and plane, are available out of Juneau or Gustavus.

Kayaking is the cheapest way to go, if time is available and the kayaker can get his craft to the bay. (Few floatplanes can carry rigid boats.) Even from Hoonah (which can be reached by ferry) it's a two-day paddle across Icy Strait, and it's 43 miles from Bartlett Cove to the nearest glacier face. Kayakers should wear life jackets, carry a tide table, stay within a quarter-mile of shore, and make for shore at a hint of wind. Pull the kayak well above tideline — remember, the tidal range is 25 feet — and make it fast to a rock or tree. Canoes are not recommended; they ride high on the water and may capsize in a sudden gust of wind. Steer clear of seabirds, seals, whales and icebergs.

Firewood is piled high at a cabin near Dundas Bay. Buck Harbeson, who came to mine in the area in the 1930s, once occupied the cabin.
(Karen Jettmar)

Two trails from Bartlett Cove offer pleasant hikes. There are no other maintained trails in the park. Hikers should carry a compass and a topographic map (available at Park Headquarters), notify a park ranger of your planned route, and never go alone. Wear sturdy boots, take plenty of insect repellent, fine-mesh

mosquito netting, warm clothing and rain gear.

Fishing: Charter boat and fishing guide services are available at the Bartlett Cove concession and in Gustavus. An Alaska fishing license is required and may be obtained at Glacier Bay Lodge or the Gustavus post office. Salmon and halibut are caught in the bay; crab and shrimp pots may be productive up-bay; some lakes and streams have cutthroat and Dolly Varden. Ask a park ranger which ones. The lodge chef will prepare and serve your catch, so will the cook at the Gustavus Inn, or have it frozen and sent home by Alaska Airlines.

Firearms are prohibited in the park; they are allowed in the preserve at Dry Bay.

Programs and services: Ranger-naturalists lead daily walks from the lodge, give scheduled slide-illustrated lectures and camper-orientation talks, board cruise and tour boats to explain the ecology of the bay and answer questions. There are daily films, and exhibits at the lodge and on the wharf. Rangers are stationed in the field but not at fixed locations where visitors can count on finding them.

Rangers and ranger-naturalists are there to interpret and protect the park and its plant and animal inhabitants, advise visitors, answer questions, and help in emergencies. They cannot be expected to protect the visitor from his own folly. The key to successful exploration in Glacier Bay is to be experienced, knowledgeable and self-reliant in the out-of-doors, or leave the responsibilities to cruise-ship personnel.

Photographer George Wuerthner lands a lively Dolly Varden at Berg Cove.
(Courtesy of George Wuerthner)

Hazards to Guard Against

Mosquitoes and other biting insects, though seldom bothersome on the water, can make hiking and camping miserable. Remember insect repellent and fine-mesh mosquito netting.

All bears should be considered dangerous. Get the *Bear Warning* leaflet at Park Headquarters and study it. Avoid bears if you can. Stay on open ground as much as possible, keep watch, stay upwind of a bear if you see one. Talk, sing, whistle or hang bells on yourself when you're hiking, to let the bear know you're around (all bears are short-sighted), and they'll probably avoid you.

Meltwater streams are turbulent and some carry so much glacial silt that you can't see bottom. They're shallower in the morning, as melt slows during the night. Wider places are usually shallower. Loosen the waist-strap of your pack so you can slip it off if you must; leave your boots on to reduce the danger of slipping; use a stout stick for balance, and angle slightly downstream.

Use your stick to test the ground ahead when you're walking on glacial moraine. Unsolidified drift can act like quicksand. Keep a respectful distance from a glacier face. Ice could slough off and bury you. It's safer to stay off a glacier surface, but it you must walk on it, test every step before you take it. And remember, ice caves are potential death traps.

Relevant addresses:

Glacier Bay National Park & Preserve, Superintendent, Gustavus, Alaska 99826. (907) 697-3341.

Juneau Chamber of Commerce, 1107 W. 8th St., Juneau, Alaska 99801. (907) 586-6420.

Selected Bibliography

ALASKA ALMANAC®, THE. Alaska Northwest Publishing Co., Edmonds, Wash., 1988.

ALASKA GEOGRAPHIC®, Alaska's Forest Resources, Vol. 12, No. 2. The Alaska Geographic Society, Anchorage, 1985.

ALASKA GEOGRAPHIC®, Alaska's Glaciers, Vol. 9, No. 1. The Alaska Geographic Society, Anchorage, 1982.

ALASKA GEOGRAPHIC®, Where Mountains Meet the Sea, Vol. 13, No. 1. The Alaska Geographic Society, Anchorage, 1986.

ALASKA WILDERNESS MILEPOST®, The. Alaska Northwest Publishing Co., Edmonds, Wash., 1988.

Armstrong, Robert H. *Guide to the Birds of Alaska.* Alaska Northwest Publishing Co., Anchorage, 1983.

Bancroft, Hubert Howe, *History of Alaska.* Antiquarian Press, New York, 1959.

Black, Bruce W. *A History of Glacier Bay National Monument Alaska.* National Park Service, 1957.

Bohn, Dave. *Glacier Bay: The Land and the Silence.* Alaska National Parks & Monuments Association, Gustavus, Alaska, 1967.

Caldwell, Francis. *Land of the Ocean Mists.* Alaska Northwest Publishing Co., Edmonds, Wash., 1986.

Cooper, William S. *A Contribution To The History Of The Glacier Bay National Monument.* Department of Botany, University of Minnesota, Minneapolis, 1956.

DuFresne, Jim. *Glacier Bay National Park.* The Mountaineers, Seattle, 1987.

Harriman Alaska Expedition, Volumes I and II. Doubleday Page Company, New York, 1899.

La Perouse, J.F. *A Voyage 'Round the World 1785-1788.* Trans. from the French. London, 1799.

Matson, Ruth O. *Happy Alaskans, We.* Goose Cove Press, San Francisco, 1972.

MILEPOST® The. Alaska Northwest Publishing Co., Edmonds, Wash., 1988.

Muir, John. *Travels In Alaska.* Houghton, Mifflin Company, Boston, 1979.

National Park Service. *Glacier Bay.* U.S. Department of the Interior, Washington, D.C., 1983.

Orth, Donald J. *Dictionary of Alaska Place Names.* Geological Survey Professional Paper 567. U.S. Government Printing Office, Washington, D.C., 1971.

Rossman, Darwin L. *Geology and Ore Deposits in the Reid Inlet Area Glacier Bay, Alaska.* Geological Survey Bulletin 1958-B. Washington, D.C.: U.S. Government Printing Office, 1958.

Vancouver, George. *A Voyage of Discovery to the North Pacific Ocean and Round the World, Performed in the Years 1790- 95.* 3 Vols. C.J. and J. Robinson; J. Edwards, London, 1798.

Alaska Geographic® Back Issues

The North Slope, Vol. 1, No. 1. Charter issue. *Out of print.*

One Man's Wilderness, Vol. 1, No. 2. A man fulfills his dream of building a cabin and living in the Bush. 116 pages, $9.95.

Admiralty . . . Island in Contention, Vol. 1, No. 3. In depth review of Southeast's Admiralty Island. 78 pages, $5.

Fisheries of the North Pacific: History, Species, Gear & Processes, Vol. 1, No. 4. *Out of print.* Book edition available.

The Alaska-Yukon Wild Flowers Guide, Vol. 2, No. 1. *Out of print.* Book edition available.

Richard Harrington's Yukon, Vol. 2, No. 2. *Out of print.*

Prince William Sound, Vol. 2, No. 3. *Out of print.*

Yakutat: The Turbulent Crescent, Vol. 2, No. 4. *Out of print.*

Glacier Bay: Old Ice, New Land, Vol. 3, No. 1. *Out of print.*

The Land: Eye of the Storm, Vol. 3, No. 2. *Out of print.*

Richard Harrington's Antarctic, Vol. 3, No. 3. Reviews Antarctica and islands of southern polar regions, territories of mystery and controversy. Fold-out map. 104 pages, $8.95.

The Silver Years of the Alaska Canned Salmon Industry: An Album of Historical Photos, Vol. 3, No. 4. *Out of print.*

Alaska's Volcanoes: Northern Link in the Ring of Fire, Vol. 4, No. 1. *Out of print.*

The Brook Range: Environmental Watershed, Vol. 4, No. 2. *Out of print.*

Kodiak: Island of Change, Vol. 4, No. 3. *Out of print.*

Wilderness Proposals: Which Way for Alaska's Lands?, Vol. 4, No. 4. *Out of print.*

Cook Inlet Country, Vol. 5, No. 1. *Out of print.*

Southeast: Alaska's Panhandle, Vol. 5, No. 2. Explores southeastern Alaska's maze of fjords and islands, forests and mountains, from Dixon Entrance to Icy Bay, including all of the Inside Passage. The book profiles every town, and reviews the region's history, economy, people, attractions and future. Fold-out map. 192 pages, $12.95.

Bristol Bay Basin, Vol. 5, No. 4. *Out of print.*

Alaska Whales and Whaling, Vol. 5, No. 4. *Out of print.*

Yukon-Kuskokwim Delta, Vol. 6, No. 1. *Out of print.*

The Aurora Borealis, Vol. 6, No. 2. Explores the northern lights in history and today; their cause, how they work, and their importance in contemporary science. 96 pages, $7.95.

Alaska's Native People, Vol. 6, No. 3. Examines the worlds of the Inupiat and Yupik Eskimo, Athabascan, Aleut, Tlingit, Haida and Tsimshian. Fold-out map of Native villages and language areas. 304 pages, $24.95.

The Stikine, Vol. 6, No. 4. River route to three Canadian gold strikes, the Stikine is the largest and most navigable of several rivers that flow from northwestern Canada through southeastern Alaska to the Pacific Ocean. Fold-out map. 96 pages, $9.95.

Alaska's Great Interior, Vol. 7, No. 1. Examines the people, communites, economy, and wilderness of Alaska's rich Interior, the immense valley between the Alaska Range and Brooks Range. Fold-out map. 128 pages, $9.95.

A Photographic Geography of Alaska, Vol. 7, No. 2. A visual tour through the six regions of Alaska: Southeast, Southcentral/Gulf Coast, Alaska Peninsula and Aleutians, Bering Sea Coast, Arctic and Interior. 192 pages, $15.95.

The Aleutians, Vol. 7, No. 3. Home of the Aleut, a tremendous wildlife spectacle, a major World War II battleground, and an important arm of Alaska's commercial fishing industry. Fold-out map. 224 pages, $14.95.

Klondike Lost: A Decade of Photographs by Kinsey & Kinsey, Vol. 7, No. 4. Pictorial review of the Klondike gold rush, focusing on the boom town of Grand Forks. 128 pages, $12.95.

Wrangell-Saint Elias, Vol. 8, No. 1. Alaska's only designated World Heritage Area, this mountain wilderness takes in the nation's largest national park in its sweep from the Copper River across the Wrangell Mountains to the southern tip of the Saint Elias Range near Yakutat. Fold-out map. 144 pages, $9.95.

Alaska Mammals, Vol. 8, No. 2. Reviews in anecdotes and facts the entire spectrum of Alaska's wildlife. 184 pages. $12.95.

The Kotzebue Basin, Vol. 8, No. 3. Examines northwestern Alaska's thriving trading area of Kotzebue Sound and the Kobuk and Noatak river basins. 184 pages. $12.95.

Alaska National Interest Lands, Vol. 8, No. 4. Reviews each of Alaska's national interest lands (d-2 lands) selections, outlining location, size, access and briefly describing special attractions. 242 pages, $14.95.

Alaska's Glaciers, Vol. 9, No. 1. *Out of print.*

Sitka and Its Ocean/Island World, Vol. 9, No. 2. *Out of print.*

Islands of the Seals: The Pribilofs, Vol. 9, No. 3. Great herds of northern fur seals and immense flocks of seabirds share their island homeland with Aleuts brought to this remote Bering Sea outpost by Russians. 128 pages, $9.95.

Alaska's Oil/Gas & Minerals Industry, Vol. 9, No. 4. Experts detail the geological processes and resulting mineral and fossil fuel resources that contribute substantially to Alaska's economy. 216 pages, $12.95.

Adventure Roads North: The Story of the Alaska Highway and Other Roads in *The MILEPOST®*, **Vol. 10, No. 1.** Reviews the history of Alaska's roads and takes a mile-by-mile look at the country they cross. 224 pages, $14.95.

ANCHORAGE and the Cook Inlet Basin, Vol. 10, No. 2. Reviews in depth the commercial and urban center of the Last Frontier. Three fold-out maps. 168 pages, $14.95.

Alaska's Salmon Fisheries, Vol. 10, No. 3. A comprehensive look at Alaska's most valuable commercial fishery. 128 pages, $12.95.

Up the Koyukuk, Vol. 10, No. 4. Highlights the wildlife and traditional native lifestyle of this remote region of northcentral Alaska. 152 pages, $14.95.

Nome: City of the Golden Beaches, Vol. 11, No. 1. Reviews the colorful history of one of Alaska's most famous gold rush towns. 184 pages, $14.95.

Alaska's Farms and Gardens, Vol. 11, No. 2. An overview of the past, present and future of agriculture in Alaska, with details on growing your own vegetables in the North. 144 pages, $12.95.

Chilkat River Valley, Vol. 11, No. 3. Explores the mountain-rimmed valley at the head of the Inside Passage, its natural resources, and the residents who have settled there. 112 pages, $12.95.

Alaska Steam, Vol. 11, No. 4. Pictorial history of the pioneering Alaska Steamship Company. 160 pages, $12.95.

Northwest Territories, Vol. 12, No. 1. In depth look at the magnificent wilderness of Canada's high Arctic. Fold-out map. 136 pages, $12.95.

Alaska's Forest Resources, Vol. 12, No. 2. Examines the botanical, recreational and economic value of Alaska's forests. 200 pages, $14.95.

Alaska Native Arts and Crafts, Vol. 12, No. 3. In depth review of the art and artifacts of Alaska's Natives. 215 pages, $17.95.

Our Arctic Year, Vol. 12, No. 4. Compelling story of a year in the wilds of the Brooks Range. 150 pages, $12.95.

Where Mountains Meet the Sea: Alaska's Gulf Coast, Vol. 13, No. 1. Alaskan's first-hand descriptions of the 850-mile arc that crowns the Pacific Ocean from Kodiak to Cape Spencer at the entrance to southeastern Alaska's Inside Passage. 191 pages, $14.95.

Backcountry Alaska, Vol. 13, No. 2. A full-color look at the remote communities of Alaska. Companion volume to The ALASKA WILDERNESS MILEPOST®. 224 pages, $14.95.

British Columbia's Coast/The Canadian Inside Passage, Vol. 13, No. 3. Reviews the B.C. coast west of the Coast Mountain divide from mighty Vancouver and elegant Victoria in the south to the forested wilderness to the north, including the Queen Charlotte Islands. Fold-out map. 200 pages, $14.95.

Lake Clark/Lake Iliamna Country, Vol. 13, No. 4. Chronicles the human and natural history of the region that many claim has a sampling of all the best that Alaska has to offer in natural beauty. 152 pages, $14.95.

Dogs of the North, Vol. 14, No. 1. *Out of print.*

South/Southeast Alaska, Vol. 14, No. 2. Reviews the natural and human resources of the southernmost tip of Alaska's Panhandle, from Sumner Strait to the Canadian border. Fold-out map. 120 pages, $14.95.

Alaska's Seward Peninsula, Vol. 14, No. 3. The Seward Peninsula is today's remnant of the Bering Land Bridge, gateway to an ancient America. This issue chronicles the blending of traditional Eskimo culture with the white man's persistent search for gold on a remote peninsula where continental North America reaches its westernmost extent, and offshore on Saint Lawrence Island, only toehold for the Siberian Yupik people in the western world. Fold-out map. 112 pages, $14.95.

The Upper Yukon Basin, Vol. 14, No. 4, 1987. Headwaters for one of the continent's mightiest rivers and gateway for some of Alaska's earliest pioneers, the Upper Yukon Basin lies nestled between the mountains along the Yukon Territory-Northwest Territories border and the giants of the coastal Saint Elias Range. Yukoner Monty Alford describes this remote corner of the continent where the fur trade, mining and tourism have provided a livelihood for the less than 30,000 hardy settlers. Illustrated with contemporary color and historical black-and-white photographs. U.S. $14.95; Canada, $18.95.

NEXT ISSUE:
Dawson City, Vol. 15, No. 2, Anchorage writer Mike Doogan traces the history of Dawson City from the chaos of the Klondike Gold Rush through the post-rush decline and up to the present. The readable text begins with a simple discussion of the region's geology, including why the area is rich in minerals, and continues with sections on such subjects as Natives, early explorers, the mining life, Dawson society and more. Heavily illustrated with historical black-and-white and contemporary color photos. To members in May 1988; price to be announced.

ALL PRICES SUBJECT TO CHANGE.

Your $30 membership in The Alaska Geographic Society includes four subsequent issues of *ALASKA GEOGRAPHIC®*, the Society's official quarterly. Please add $4 for non-U.S. membership.

Additional membership information is available upon request. Single copies of the *ALASKA GEOGRAPHIC®* back issues are also available. When ordering, please make payments in U.S. funds and add $1 postage/handling per copy. To order back issues send your check or money order and volumes desired to:

The Alaska Geographic Society

P.O. Box 93370, Anchorage, Alaska 99509